Strength and stamina training

This book is a new version, with much additional material, of the author's earlier work *Training with weights*

To my father for stimulating my interest in exercise and writing,
and to my mother for the many ways in which she has helped

Printed in Great Britain by Jarrold and Sons Ltd, Norwich

0 7195 1999 3

Eric Taylor

Strength and stamina training

A guide to training with weights, circuit training and isometric exercise

John Murray

Contents

Preface

SIX MAJOR physiological and psychological factors influence success in sport and athletics: strength, stamina, skill, speed, agility and the will to win. And of all these, the most easily developed are strength and stamina. With this development there is almost bound to be an improvement in performance, especially during the early stages of training.

For some years world-class athletes have recognised the need for strength and stamina training. Women as well as men have trained with weights, used rubber and springs as resistance, practised isometric exercises at odd times during the day and followed rigorous circuit training schedules to prepare themselves physically for fierce competition. It is not news.

But what is of interest today is the way sportsmen and athletes of smaller clubs, people who play for pleasure, have realised that more enjoyment and satisfaction can be gained from sport by developing strength and stamina.

With greater strength comes increased power, a combination of strength and speed, and with greater reserves of stamina comes improvement of skill because the onset of fatigue is delayed. When muscles are fatigued, they send out signals of pain and discomfort which distract the performer. Concentration wanes and errors are made. Accuracy is lost and a greater conscious effort is needed to carry out movements which at the beginning of play would have been done instinctively. A higher level of muscular strength and endurance almost invariably produces an improved and more consistent standard of play.

Obviously different sports and athletic events require varying degrees of strength and stamina and no two individuals are alike in their needs for physical development, but it is possible to provide a basic guide to training programmes once the activity has been analysed and the individual's strength assessed.

This book attempts to provide the individual, coach, and schoolmaster with a practical guide to strength and stamina training schedules using weights, isometric exercise and circuit training.

Theoretical discussion has been kept to the minimum, but in order to help individuals training without the help of a qualified coach or physical education specialist some physiological explanations have been included.

I would like to thank the athletes and sportsmen who have co-operated in the research into training methods, and in particular I want to thank Mr Norman Creek of the Football Association for the opportunity of giving fitness training to the British Olympic Soccer team, Herr Rolf Furtwangler of the Institute of Sports Medicine, Munster

University, for his help in providing research papers and advice on current developments in physical education and Mr David Rooney, Headmaster of King's School, Gütersloh, for his help and encouragement.

Here, also, I would like to thank Beryl, my wife, for her encouragement and patience whilst the book was being written.

Acknowledgments

Acknowledgments are due to the following for their kind permission to reproduce copyright material:

The demonstration photographs in chapter 4 and those of the female models in chapters 6, 13, 14 and 15—Stanley Wigmore; p. 66—*Pressbild Agentur Schirner*; p. 98—Ron Pickering (from his book *Strength Training for Athletics* (A.A.A.)); p. 213—Keystone Press Agency. The diagrams on pp. 216–18 are based on illustrations in *A.P. 3125* (H.M.S.O.) by permission of the controller.
I am also most grateful to Mike Johns, Keith Pritchard and Mike Beadle for their help and advice with the photographs for isometric exercises and circuit training.

1 Training for strength

TRAINING IS always more effective when the aim is clear. What is strength? It has often been defined as the capacity of muscles to exert a force against resistance. Within this meaning fatigue does not affect the force that can be exerted in one maximum effort. But once we consider the capacity of muscles to continue exerting a force against resistance, fatigue becomes an important factor. We are then concerned with stamina: the efficiency of the circulatory and respiratory systems plus determination or will-power.

Muscular strength may be developed by exercising muscles against a resistance that is gradually increased; this is generally known as the 'principle of overload' or 'progressive resistance'. Usually this resistance is provided by weights, springs or rubber strands. Strength may also be developed by making muscles work maximally against a fixed resistance; this method, which has been given much publicity in recent years, is known as isometric exercise.

Muscular endurance is developed by exercising muscles vigorously over an increasingly longer period of time so that more work is done before fatigue impairs performance. It is important to recognise the difference between strength and stamina when training schedules are being prepared.

Progressive resistance exercise

Pick up a pen and only a few fibres of the arm flexor muscles contract. Substitute a crowbar for the pen and a much greater proportion of fibres need to work. If a heavy weight is lifted repeatedly the load is shunted from one set of fibres to another so that those which become fatigued have time to rest and recover. The heavier the weight the greater is the proportion of muscle fibres involved and therefore fewer are left to relieve those which are fatigued. Consequently, after a few repetitions with a heavy weight, the working muscles become thoroughly fatigued and incapable of further effort until they have been rested long enough to recover.

Some exercises lend themselves better than others to the application of overload because the movements can be done in exactly the same manner each time and the load easily adjusted to increase the resistance. Weight training with barbells and dumb-bells, for example, is obviously one of the most effective ways of applying a load or resistance to a muscle. It presents a challenge and is a satisfying form of exercise.

When heavy work is done at regular training sessions and the weight is gradually increased, the muscle fibres develop so that the narrow ones become broader and stronger.

Fewer fibres can then do the work previously done by many more. The development of these narrow fibres is usually described as 'hypertrophy' and training by progressively increasing the resistance is called the 'principle of overload'. Hypertrophy is a natural and beneficial development, whether it be of the skeletal or the cardiac muscles.

Isometric exercise

When the German physiologists, Professor E. A. Muller and Doctor Hettinger of the Max-Planck Institute, Dortmund, published the results of their research [1,2] into the effects of isometric exercise on strength development, recognition began to be given to a form of strength training which seemed almost too good to be true. For only a few minutes of training each week strength gains were being made which had previously only been achieved after months of strenuous weight training.

Commenting on this investigation by Muller and Hettinger, A. D. Munrow wrote:

'One can imagine the reaction of a group of trade union officials, who after months of patient bargaining have negotiated a wage agreement, hearing of a firm round the corner employing non-union labour and paying double rates for half the hours with a month's holiday with pay. I think the reaction of many of us in sport and physical education to this news from the Max-Planck Institute was similar.'[3]

Since the Muller-Hettinger reports were published, experiments have been carried out at many universities throughout the world in order to establish whether or not the claims made for isometric exercise were true or not. The reports of these experiments are generally not quite as startling as the original from the Max-Planck Institute but they nevertheless verify the fact that isometric exercise, taking only a few minutes a day, can produce significant gains in strength comparable with those achieved through much longer periods of isotonic progressive resistance exercise.

Isometric exercise defined

When a muscle develops tension but is unable to shorten its length it is said to be in a state of isometric or static contraction.

Tension within the muscle may be brought about by pitting one set of muscles against another of equal strength, as, for example, when the arm flexors try to bend the arm at the elbow whilst the extensors of the other arm push against the flexors to keep the forearm from bending; or it may be developed by making the muscle work against an immovable object. Another method of inducing tension isometrically is by contracting a muscle group to hold a position against the pull of a partner, weight or spring. The simplest way of contracting a muscle without moving its insertion or origin is, of course, by means of direct muscle control. The quadriceps, for example, can be braced isometrically when the leg is straight and the abdominals contracted until they are board hard without any alteration of muscle length.

In some isometric exercises there may be a little shortening of the muscle initially, when, for instance, a force is exerted against a short spring, elastic or partner's opposition until the resistance becomes too great to permit any further movement of the limbs or body. The muscles then work isometrically to maintain the position reached against the pull of the external force. These exercises are sometimes called 'partial' isometric and they are often regarded as a better form of strength training because muscles are more likely to reach a condition of near maximal contraction when there is a little shortening initially than when they work against an immovable object. (Details of isometric exercises and their application may be found in chapters 13 to 16.)

Which system to choose—isotonic or isometric?

There is no simple answer. Both are effective. In weight training, progress is immediately evident and there is a tremendous incentive for maintaining training. Furthermore, when the individual sees he is stronger he has the confidence to demand more from his muscles. He can overcome the psychological barrier to improved performance in the same way as milers did after Roger Bannister had beaten the bogey of the four-minute mile. In the two years following his feat there were thirteen sub-four-minute miles recorded.

Isometric exercise has many attractions. During the early stages of training two minutes of isometric exercise every other day will increase muscular strength at the same rate as it would increase with weight training. The lower the relative strength of the muscle then the more rapid will be the progress until a constant level of strength is reached. This level is sometimes called the 'limiting strength'. Once this condition has been reached then further gains require greater efforts to be made in training and probably a combination of methods will prove to be the most rewarding for the time devoted to training.

It is interesting at this point to consider the amount of time actually spent in exercise during a two-hour weight training session. A. R. Malcolm, Superintendent of Physical Education at Cambridge University Department of Human Ecology and Health, analysed how the time was utilised and found that only two and a half minutes were spent in actually lifting weights.

There can be no reason for doubting that isometric exercise schedules are effective and that they allow more time and energy for other aspects of training. A complete 'work-out' is of so short duration that fatigue does not trouble the performer and he is therefore fresh enough to spend more time on skill practice.

Another factor in favour of isometric exercise is that the schedules can be done at home or in the office without expensive apparatus.

However, we must acknowledge the fact that there is still a lot we do not know about the best methods of influencing strength development and furthermore we must admit that the dividing line between isometric and isotonic exercise is not always clear. For example, the weight trainer who fails to lift a heavy bar through the full range of the exercise begins to work his muscles isometrically as soon as the weight slows to a stop.

In the end the choice rests with the individual. Many enthusiasts favour a combination of isometric and isotonic exercise but whatever system is chosen the crucial fact is that the individual must believe whole-heartedly in the training programme he chooses so that he follows it conscientiously.

How safe is isometric exercise?

There is a tendency to hold the breath when isometric contractions are made and this could be harmful in the same way that breath holding when lifting weights can be dangerous due to the phenomenon of Valsalva which is explained on page 63.

Recent research has shown that care must be taken with isometric exercise, especially when practised by those with a known weakness of the heart. 'Isometric contractions,' says Dr A. L. Muir of Edinburgh University, 'throw an increased pressure load on the heart and this exerts an acute ventricular load which could be dangerous.'

Skill to utilise strength

Finally it must be recognised that additional strength has no value unless it is employed effectively; it must be integrated into the skill of the performance. It is for this reason that the chapters on skill have been included in this book.

REFERENCES

1 *Internationale Zeitschrift fur angewandte Physiologie* (19: 1963).
2 T. Hettinger, *Physiology of Strength* (C. C. Thomas, 1961).
3 A. D. Munrow, *Pure and Applied Gymnastics* (Edward Arnold).

2 Warming-up

BEFORE EVERY training session or competition a thorough warming-up routine is essential. Jog-trotting and light exercises done in warm clothing should be the prelude to the more vigorous work to follow. Warming-up exercises are not effective unless they promote a general warmth and free perspiration accompanied by an increase in the rate and depth of respiration.

Apart from warming-up the body, exercises should stretch the primary muscle groups and work joints through their full range of movement.

In addition to the jog-trotting and warming-up exercises described below, many coaches recommend a light weight lifting programme before the serious training begins.

There is still a lot we don't know about warming-up, but recent research suggests that muscles work more efficiently when the body temperature rises above normal. This happens during strenuous exercise, not because the heat-regulating mechanism fails to cope with the generation of heat in the expenditure of energy, but because of an over-riding natural phenomenon which permits temperature to rise the extra few degrees needed for efficient muscular performance. Experiments in which the body has been warmed artificially by short-wave diathermy and hot baths have tended to show that this is not as beneficial to the performance of the athlete as warming-up exercises.

Suggested programme of warming-up exercises

All the following exercises should be done freely with a relaxed and easy rhythm.

1 Jog round the gym or running track.

2 *Double arm circling:* Stand with the feet astride and swing your arms loosely overhead passing close to the ears, behind the line of the shoulders and forward again. Keep your wrists, elbows and shoulders relaxed the whole time.

3 *Single arm circling:* Place the left leg forward, slightly bent, and rest the left hand on the forward knee supporting the weight of the body in a forward-leaning position. Now circle the free arm loosely backwards and then change to swinging it forwards.

4 *Trunk and arm circling:* Feet astride, arms loosely clasped in front of the body. Swing the arms to the side, overhead, and bend the body sideways at the hips. Continue the

movement in a big circle sweeping the clasped hands across the feet and upwards again.

5 *Trunk twisting:* Stand astride, arms forward with fingers lightly clenched. Keeping the body upright, twist round to the left and then to the right. Allow the arms to swing round with the body and turn the head to look as far round as you can. Maintain the arms at shoulder height to avoid bending at the hips.

6 *Ski swings:* Feet about six inches apart. Swing the arms loosely and rhythmically backwards, forwards and upwards, at the same time bending and stretching the knees as in the ski-ing movement.

7 *Skip jumping:* Feet together, jumping upwards on the spot to land lightly with a slight bend of the ankles, knees and hips.

8 *Straight leg swinging:* Stand with one leg close to a wall and the outside leg raised off the ground so that it can be swung easily forwards and backwards. Maintain your balance by resting one hand against the wall.

9 *Knee hugging:* Stand on one leg. Raise the other, pulling the knee close to the chest. Change legs.

10 *Neck rotation:* Drop the head on to the chest, circle

over the left shoulder, backwards, upwards and down over the right shoulder.

11 *Squat thrusts:* Crouch position, knees fully bent, hands outside and a little forward of feet. Jump the left and right legs backwards and forwards alternately.

Remember, failure to warm up can be dangerous. It is easier to pull a muscle than to repair it.

Cooling-down

After a taxing heavy routine, a cooling-down session is advisable to restore the heart and breathing rate to near normal. A few minutes of light exercise will prove most beneficial in this respect and, at the same time, the squeezing action of the working muscles on the capillaries and veins will help to eliminate the by-products of fatigue and thus avoid any subsequent stiffness and soreness in the muscles and joints.

3 Methods of weight training

ALTHOUGH WIDESPREAD agreement exists about the benefits to be gained from weight training, there is a great divergence of opinion about methods. Perhaps it is because so many factors affect success that it is difficult to evaluate the importance of each one. Training records clearly show the time spent, poundage and repetitions used in a weight training schedule but there is no means of measuring the quality of determination and enthusiasm poured into the effort to succeed. No one can estimate the effect of this motivating force which drives men out for a training run on dark, wet blustery nights and to persevere with weight training schedules despite the demands made on their time by studies, career or a young family. One thing is sure, whatever the training method, success will come only when the will-power is there too.

But before attempting any weight training routine the safety precautions for handling weights must be thoroughly understood. They are simple but very important and apply to all age groups. The basic safety rules are:

1 Warm up thoroughly with general mobilising exercises before touching any weights.

2 Stop doing any exercise at the first sign of physical distress. Struggling with jerky movements to make one more repetition must be forbidden.

3 Breathe freely throughout all movements of an exercise. (See page 63 for explanation of Valsalva phenomenon.)

4 Keep the back straight and body evenly balanced over feet placed usually about twelve inches apart and flat on the floor, making a firm base.

5 Progress gradually in both repetitions and poundage.

6 Take care that locking nuts are fully tightened.

It is also worth mentioning here the risks involved in lifting heavy weights with the knee fully flexed. The full squat exercise with heavy barbell, for example, throws a damaging strain on the internal structures of the knee joint itself and consequently is not included in this book.

There are many ways of applying progressive resistance with weights. Some of them have been given a name and are recognised as a system. In the early stages of training it does not matter much which system is used but later one of them, and special techniques and advanced training methods, may be needed to maintain progress in strength or stamina development. Some of these systems and the basic methods are explained below, with the reservation that the criterion is success, and that no two men or boys are alike. If, by trial and error, one method appears to be more successful than another then that is the one to use for there is still a great deal about muscle development we need to learn. The choice of method may also depend upon whether an athlete is working by himself or as part of a group.

The three sets method

This method is favoured by the individual working with only one set of weights.

By doing three sets, one after the other, there is no need to adjust the poundage on the bar until he begins the next exercise.

Three sets of repetitions are done with only a short rest in between each set. The number of repetitions depends upon whether the aim is strength or stamina.

A poundage heavy enough to keep the maximum repetitions possible below ten is normally used for strength development, and a lighter poundage, allowing thirty or more rapid repetitions, for stamina.

Many coaches stress the importance of relaxing muscles in between each bout of exercise in order to give the circulatory system a better chance of eliminating the waste products of fatigue and speeding recovery. This relaxation

period need be no longer than about a minute and the time taken to adjust the weights for the next exercise. Arms and legs should be shaken loosely whilst lungs are ventilated with a few deeper breaths. This three sets method taxes muscle groups more severely than the sequence method and there is likely to be a more positive reaction in muscle development. Care should be taken to progress gradually and to avoid over-exertion in completing the third set. No one should tackle more repetitions in the third set once the movements have become jerky and uneven.

The sequence method

A balanced schedule for general fitness would include at least one exercise for each of the muscle groups under which exercises are classified on pages 15 to 61 and one or two for general endurance. Exercises should be done in the same order as the classifications are listed, so as to avoid taxing adjacent muscles in successive exercises.

Usually the weight recommended is one allowing no more than ten repetitions and with the sequence method a full set of ten should be done before passing on to the next exercise. At the end of each fortnight of training, there should be a testing period during which the individual should attempt his maximum performance at each exercise. If there is a marked increase beyond ten, then a little more weight can be added to the bar. But it is better to err on the safe side than to add too much weight. As always, the safe guide is form. When style is jerky or poor with six or seven repetitions some weight should be removed.

The chief disadvantage of the sequence method is that the weights on the bar must be adjusted after each exercise set, unless training is done in a gymnasium with sufficient weight training equipment to allow bars to be prepared for every exercise in the schedule without the need for poundage alterations during the routine.

Progress in weight training

Progression may be made by:
1 Increasing the number of repetitions in each set.
2 Increasing the repetitions daily and weight weekly.
3 Increasing the number of sets.
4 Increasing the weight with sets of diminishing repetitions.
5 Using a heavy and light routine.

Ideally a complete record should be made of all changes in the training programme so that progress may be easily seen and modifications made if they become necessary.

1 *Progression by increasing the repetitions in the set:* A safe but effective way of making progress is by increasing the number of repetitions in each set weekly and yet trying to complete the whole schedule in the same time. By speeding up the movements the overload effect is increased due to muscles having to check momentum and change the direction of the movement. The important principle in all progressive resistance training is to exercise muscles as thoroughly as possible by working them intensely within a short period of time.

2 *Progression by increasing repetitions daily and weight weekly:* One significant advantage of this double progression is that daily progress is possible as well as weekly (if the individual trains every day). On the first training day a trainee would complete the schedule as planned and then on successive days he would gradually increase the repetitions in each set. The ability to increase the number of repetitions indicates a corresponding increase in strength. In the early stages of training more repetitions may be possible because of improvement in the technique of the movement—getting the 'knack' of the exercise.

By the end of a week an individual in daily training who could initially do only seven arm curls in three sets, may have progressed to three sets of ten repetitions. This is the time for more weight to be added to reduce the repetitions. They can be increased as training gradually continues.

This two-pronged progression is an ideal way of developing stamina as well as strength.

3 *Progression by increasing the number of sets:* Weight trainers using this method handle the same poundages for the exercises throughout the week but as each day passes they try to build up an extra set. For example, on day 2 they may do three sets of ten squats and a fourth set of two.

Gradually the fourth set can be increased to ten and the weight would then be increased. This more severe type of training should only be undertaken by those who are already physically very strong and then only if there is a particular need for extra strength.

4 *Progression by increasing the weight with diminishing repetitions:* This method is definitely only for advanced weight training schedules. The target with the diminishing repetitions routine is to work up to one supreme lift of the heaviest weight possible for the exercise. Advanced weight trainers start with a weight that can be lifted four or five times, then for the second set more weight is added which perhaps permits only two repetitions and, finally, yet more weight is added so that the exercise can only be done once. The object of the diminishing repetitions method is to elicit maximal contraction for the final movement. If the weight for the third set has not been judged accurately, more weight again can be added for a single lift.

5 *Progression by the heavy and light routine:* Two barbells are loaded for each exercise. One barbell has a very heavy load and the other a comparatively light one. Then alternate sets of repetitions are done with the heavy and light poundages until three sets of each have been completed. As strength and endurance improve, more weight can be added to the lighter barbell and then to the heavier. The theory behind this routine is that the use of a lighter load between the heavy sets permits a degree of muscular recovery and that with three sets of each a greater percentage of muscle fibres can be exercised strenuously within a given period of time.

Progress during the early stages of weight training is always rapid. It comes from a threefold improvement. First of all there is 'motor learning', when you get the feeling of the movement and can do it with less effort. Then there is an improvement in nervous co-ordination so that a greater proportion of muscle fibres can be contracted by the same nervous stimulus. And finally comes the true progression in strength, stemming from muscular development.

This threefold improvement helps to explain the dramatic progress which delights the weight trainer during the early weeks of training. Then as training proceeds, progress becomes increasingly more difficult to achieve.

But before embarking upon any of the advanced training routines the questions must be asked, 'How strong do I want to be?' and 'Could the time be more profitably spent on skill development or tactical training?' There is little to be gained from going willy-nilly after greater and greater strength, for after a certain level has been reached progress becomes more difficult and a disproportionate amount of training is necessary for continued progress.

It is up to the teacher or coach to decide, in discussion with the individual, how much strength is really required. The decision will depend upon the time available and the need for extra strength or muscular development.

Equipment you need to buy

You don't need to buy a lot of costly equipment to start weight training. The catalogues and muscle magazines display a wide variety of weights and apparatus, some of which is very expensive, but for about £8 the beginner can buy enough to meet all his needs.

The sportsman, athlete, or individual training for basic fitness can manage well enough without recourse to 'lat' machines, leg press machines, or expensive adjustable benches. The routines recommended in this book have been selected with the practical consideration of cost in mind.

This is all the beginner needs to buy:

Bar, 4 feet 6 inches		1
Dumb-bell rods, 15 inches ..		2
Collars		8
Discs		120 lb

    5 lb × 4....20 lb
    10 lb × 4....40 lb
    15 lb × 4....60 lb

Suppliers vary a little in price and it is worthwhile looking at more than one catalogue.

Cutting the cost

If you buy second-hand the cost can be more than halved. Equipment does not wear out. Locking nuts may rust if they have been left in the corner of a garage, and bars may become rough and pitted, but new nuts can be bought and sleeves fitted over the rods to provide a smooth grip. (A rough bar can soon raise blisters on your hands.)

Magazines such as *Health and Strength*, and *Exchange and Mart* often carry advertisements of second-hand equipment for sale but transport costs are high and these should be considered when agreement is reached on the price, if the purchaser has to arrange collection.

Storage

Another factor to be considered is the storage of the equipment when not in use. Home trainers can roll dumb-bells and barbells under the bed. There is no problem until such items as squat stands and benches are bought. Don't buy them until you feel it is really necessary.

The value of additional items of equipment

There is usually a reason for buying additional equipment other than whim or to introduce variety into the training programme, for this equipment is expensive enough to cause even the most affluent and fanatical weight trainer to think twice. The merits of some of the better-known pieces of equipment are discussed below.

Iron boots: Iron boots cost about £2 a pair and are used mainly for two reasons. To develop the extensor muscles of the thigh and to provide hard work for the abdominal muscles. The vastus medialis muscle, which runs along the inside and front of the thigh, contracts most strongly during the last fifteen degrees of extension of the knee. It straightens the leg out fully. In the half squat exercise, when the knees are extended from a half bent position, the vastus medialis can shunt a lot of the effort on to the other parts of the quadriceps muscle, and so a more specific exercise must be done if the full development of the vastus medialis is to be achieved.

Furthermore, squats also develop the gluteals of the buttocks especially if the body is bent forward at the hips during the raise from the knees full bend position (but see warning on page 7). If thigh development without gluteal work is needed then the knee extension exercise is the one to be done, and for this iron boots are essential. The boots

resemble a shoe without a top and have a hole in the base below the instep to carry a loaded dumb-bell bar.

For abdominal development their value is doubtful. Inclined trunk curls and twists with the curl are still the better forms of exercise.

Benches: Many of the chest as well as the abdominal exercises are performed from a bench or an inclined bench. A bench is useful for the chest exercises because it allows the shoulders and arms to hang below the level of the chest thus working the pectoral muscles of the upper chest from a lengthened position. But before rushing out to buy a bench think of the alternatives. Improvise by placing a board between two chairs so that there is enough room for you to lie straddling the supporting board whilst your arms hang below shoulder level. Even if a bench cannot be found or improvised, the exercises are still effective if done from a lying position on the floor.

Inclined trunk curls are really only possible on a strong bench but again there is no need to buy. A bench can easily be made to satisfy most of the requirements. For the 'do it yourself' handymen a photograph of one that has proved most serviceable is shown on page 16.

'Lat' machines: It is difficult to exercise the latissimus dorsi from the standing position. The function of this muscle is to pull your arms downwards to the sides of the body. The 'lats' are used in heaves on the bar, as you chin yourself,

and in breast-stroke swimming. The 'lat' machine provides resistance through pulleys as the handles are pulled down to lift the weight on the end of the wire as shown below.

trainer lies on his back, presses his feet against the loaded platform and extends his knees.

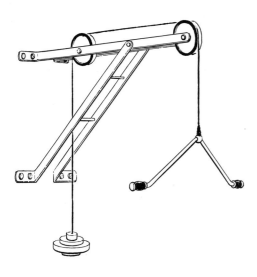

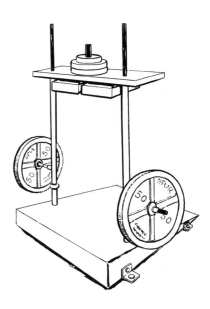

Only advanced weight trainers should consider the use of this machine as essential. It is effective but hardly worth the additional expense (about £10) unless excessive latissimus dorsi strength is needed.

Leg pressing machine: This is another piece of equipment found in well-appointed gymnasia but not essential. The

It needs little thought to realise that for the leg muscles there is an adequate supply of exercises without having to spend £15 for one of these machines. But the enthusiastic body builders are fond of the leg press machine; it is easy to load and safe to use with heavy weights.

Calf machine: The heel-raise exercise is often done with the calf machine in order to employ very heavy weights in the small range of movement possible with this exercise. It costs about £10 but again the handyman can soon make himself an admirable substitute. The diagram below shows the machine manufactured by George Grose Ltd.

Squat stands: When very heavy weights are used, the bar can be loaded on the squat stands so that the individual training alone can place the bar accurately on his shoulders and lift it with a straight back before beginning the exercise. He can also release the weight on to the supporting stands after finishing the set number of repetitions without staggering about to lower the heavy bar to the ground. Injuries can often result from unsteady releases with a rounded back.

From time to time new developments in equipment become available and advice on these additional items can be obtained from qualified coaches. A 'revolving sleeve' and a 'power rack' for example are well worth considering by those aiming for a well-equipped gymnasium.

4 Weight training exercises for the major muscle groups

MAINLY FOR THE ELBOW FLEXORS

1 *Arm curls:* Stand with the feet a little apart and hold the barbell with the palms of the hands forward, arms hanging straight down and the bar lying across the front of the thighs. Bend your elbows to bring the bar up to the shoulder. If you want to put more work on to the shoulder flexors, push the bar forward a little before bending the elbows, thereby causing more effort to be made by the anterior fibres of the deltoids.

2 *Inclined bench barbell curls:* Lie on an inclined bench at about forty-five degrees, the head higher than the rest of the body and holding the bar as for the previous exercise. Curl the bar up to the shoulder. The modified starting position on the bench will make it less easy for other muscle groups to give assistance to the curl and thereby take some of the load from the elbow flexors. For example, when the curl is done from the standing position there is a tendency for the back to be hollowed and the hips swung forward to bring into play the powerful short muscles of the lumbar region which assist the biceps and brachialis.

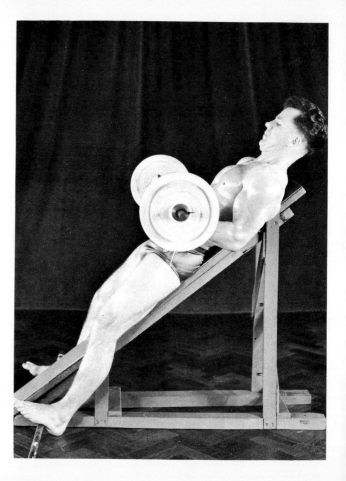

3 *Seated half curls:* This exercise is used to allow a heavier weight to be handled from the starting position in which the arm flexors, being already in a shortened condition, begin to work at a mechanical advantage. When the elbows are straight it takes a much greater effort to bend them than when they are partly bent. Rest the barbell across the thighs and grasp it with the hands just outside the legs. Curl the bar up to the shoulder as with the other curls.

4 *Single arm curls supported:* Rest the upper arm on the inclined bench. Curl the bar to the shoulder. Again, with this starting position, the movement is confined to the elbow flexors and it is impossible to cheat by bringing in other muscle groups (see right).

5 *Reverse curls:* Grasp the barbell with overgrip, the palms towards the thighs. Tuck the elbows firmly into the waist and curl the barbell up to the shoulder.

6 *Alternate arm curls:* Stand astride, leaning forward slightly at the hips, arms hanging loosely in front of the body, holding a dumb-bell in each hand with the thumbs to the front. Alternately bend the left and the right arms bringing the weight up to the shoulder.

7 *Cheating barbell curls:* Use a much heavier poundage than for the simple arm curl. Give a rhythmical swing back at the hips to give impetus to the initial movement of the curl. Make sure that you have a firm base with the feet about twelve inches apart.

8 *Bench end barbell curls:* Lie face downwards on the bench so that your shoulders just project over the end. Allow the weight to rest on the floor and then curl it up to the shoulders. Lower down slowly so as to work the flexors eccentrically in a lengthening condition.

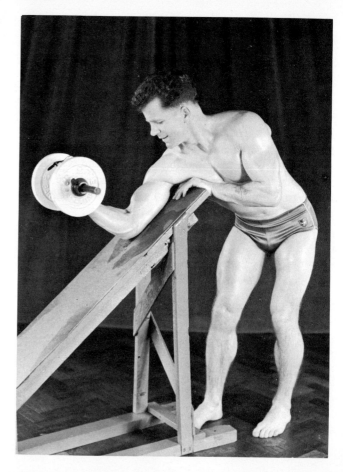

9 *Arms raising forwards and sideways:* This exercise is mainly for the frontal and mid fibres of the deltoids. The best effects are gained from a steady straight arm lift rather than from a rhythmical swinging movement. Hold the dumb-bells by the side and raise the arms sideways and lower down, raise them now forwards and lower down.

10 *Arms forwards and upwards raise:* This is a good exercise for warming up. Hold the dumb-bell in front of the thighs with the hands shoulder width apart and the thumbs towards each other. Swing the bar forwards and upwards above the head. Lower slowly and repeat. The weight should be light enough for the exercise to be done by the arm and shoulder muscles without recourse to bending of the hips, knees or loin to give the initial impetus.

11 *Chinning, clasped hands grasp:* Use the grip as shown on the right. Pull up until the face is alongside the bar.

12 *Chinning:* Grasp the horizontal bar or beam above stretch height. Pull up until the chin is over the top of the bar. If the exercise is done with an undergrasp, that is, with the palms facing the body, then most of the muscle work is done by the pectorals. But if a wide overgrasp is used (palms away) and the elbows pressed well back, the main effort is thrown upon the latissimus dorsi muscle. The grip therefore should be varied during training. The photographs on the left show chinning over the bar and chinning with the bar behind the neck for more dorsal effect.

MAINLY FOR THE SHOULDER FLEXORS AND ABDUCTORS

These exercises develop the frontal and middle fibres of the deltoids and the trapezius muscle.

1 *High pull-up to stretch position:* Grasp the barbell with the hands about six inches apart. Keeping the body erect, pull the bar up, passing close to the body and face until it is in the stretch position above the head. Start with a lighter weight at first until you get the feel of the movement and can do it without strain.

2 *Upright rowing:* Use a narrow grip for this exercise. By bending the arms at the elbows and allowing the wrist to drop, lift the barbell to chin height and pause for the count of five. Lower the bar, slowly pressing the shoulder blades together all the time.

 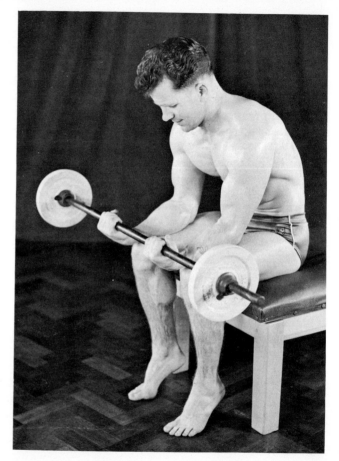

3 *Shoulder shrugging:* Hold a heavy dumb-bell in each hand by the side of the thighs. Raise the shoulders as high as you can and then press them backwards squeezing the shoulder blades together. Let them drop and then thrust them forward and upwards again.

FOREARM EXERCISES

1 *Winding the weight:* Pass one end of a piece of cord through the hole in a disc. Tie the other end round an oval-shaped bar (or better still drill a hole through a wooden bar and pass the cord through the hole before tying). Hold the bar with the weight suspended below and then by twisting the bar, wind up the cord which raises the weight.

2 *The wrist curl:* Hold the barbell as shown on the left with the forearm resting on the thigh and the wrist protruding beyond the knee. Flex the wrist upwards and towards the body. Avoid bending the elbow.

3 *Reverse wrist curl:* Hold the weight with the palms towards the floor and the forearm resting on the thigh as in the previous exercise. Pull the fist back as far as possible and lower down until the wrist is fully flexed.

4 *Ulnar deviation:* Stand holding the unweighted end of the dumb-bell as on the right with the thumb to the front. Bend the wrist to raise the weighted end towards the elbow.

This is a pure wrist movement used mainly by body builders requiring more precise definition of the forearm muscles and by sportsmen needing extra strength of the wrist, as for example in tennis and basketball.

5 *Radial deviation:* This again is a special exercise for definition and strength in a particular group of forearm muscles. Rest the forearm on the thigh or bench with the wrist protruding over the edge, as shown on the left. Bend the wrist keeping the thumb on top, to bring the weighted end towards the upper arm.

6 *Lever rotation:* Grasp the dumb-bell rod as shown on the right and circle the weighted end around the fist and close to the elbow joint.

There are many other exercises for the forearm that can be done at odd times of the day. Carry a rubber ball in your pocket or a Terry spring; squeeze it for as many repetitions as possible, half a dozen times a day. Another well-known trick is to take hold of the corner of a sheet of newspaper on the table and by gathering it in with the fingers of one hand squeeze it into a tight ball. Keep the forearm fixed in one place on the table throughout the exercise.

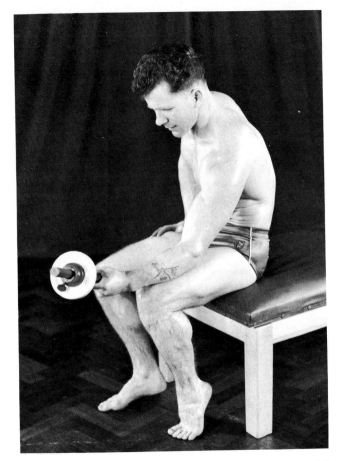

EXERCISES FOR THE ARM AND SHOULDER EXTENSORS

1 *Standing single arm triceps extension:* Hold the dumb-bell behind the shoulder. Keep the upper arm as vertical as possible and the elbow pressed close to the side of the head. Straighten your elbow until the arm is stretched upwards above the shoulder.

2 *Standing triceps extension with barbell:* Use a narrow grip on the bar and do the exercise in the same manner as described for the single arm extension above.

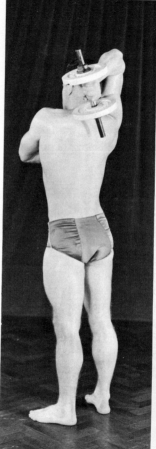
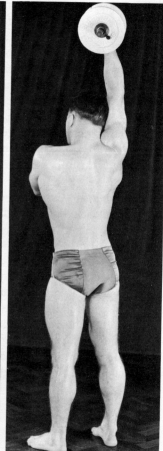

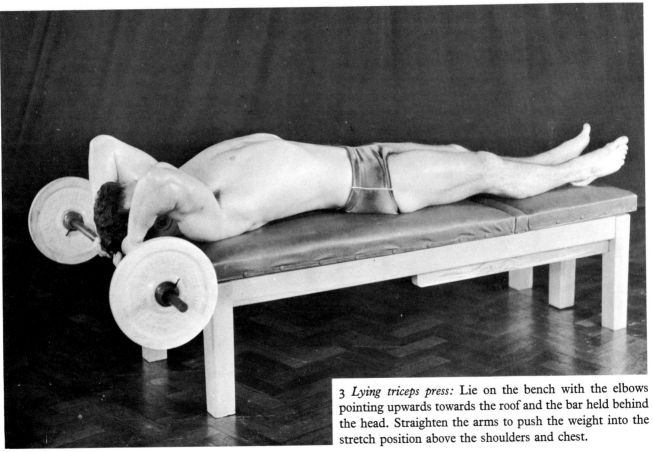

3 *Lying triceps press:* Lie on the bench with the elbows pointing upwards towards the roof and the bar held behind the head. Straighten the arms to push the weight into the stretch position above the shoulders and chest.

4 *Lying triceps extension:* Lie on the bench holding the barbell with a close grip as shown here. Stretch the arms until they are parallel with the floor and in line with the bench, as on page 29.

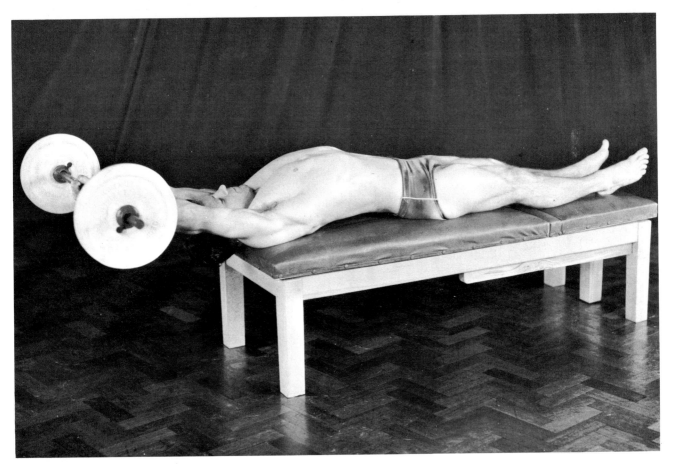

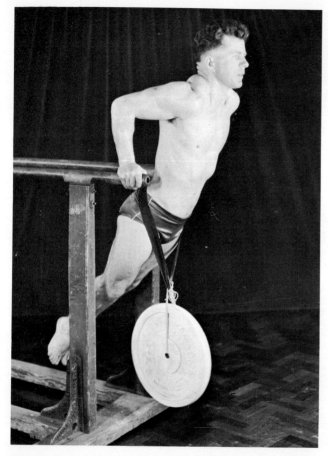

5 *Parallel bar dips:* Support the weight of the body entirely on the arms between the parallel bars, as on the left. Notice in the illustration that the weight is suspended from the waist belt but this is only to be used in the very late stages of training. Bend the arms to a right angle at the elbow and push up to the straight arm position again.

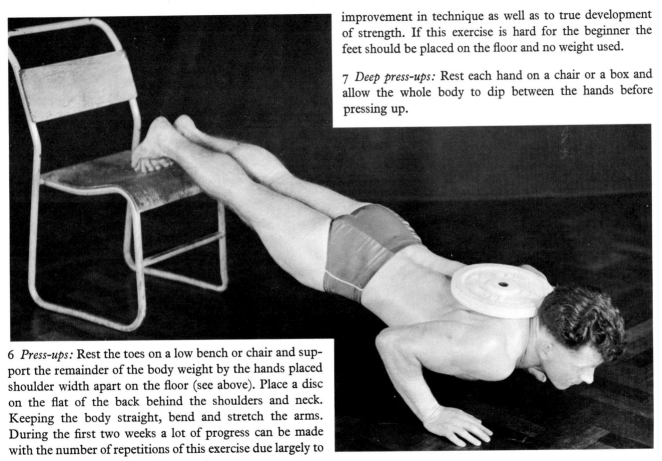

improvement in technique as well as to true development of strength. If this exercise is hard for the beginner the feet should be placed on the floor and no weight used.

7 *Deep press-ups:* Rest each hand on a chair or a box and allow the whole body to dip between the hands before pressing up.

6 *Press-ups:* Rest the toes on a low bench or chair and support the remainder of the body weight by the hands placed shoulder width apart on the floor (see above). Place a disc on the flat of the back behind the shoulders and neck. Keeping the body straight, bend and stretch the arms. During the first two weeks a lot of progress can be made with the number of repetitions of this exercise due largely to

8 *Backward press:* Stand with the barbell held behind the buttocks, palms away from the body. Keeping the elbows straight, press the weight as far back as possible.

9 *Single arm backwards press:* Stand in the forward lean position with one hand resting on the forward knee, back straight. Press the dumb-bell backwards and upwards. Lower and repeat in a steady and controlled movement, not a swing. This is a good exercise for developing the posterior fibres of the deltoids.

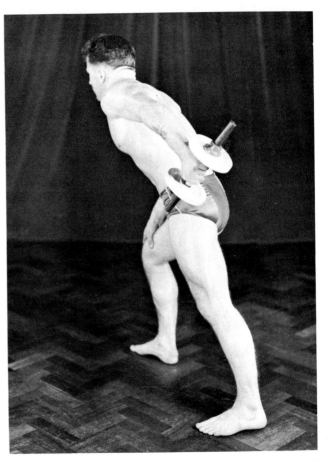

10 *Press behind the neck:* Hold the bar across the back of the neck and shoulders as shown on the left. Press upwards to the stretch position and lower slowly behind the neck. Care should be taken not to bruise the spine by allowing the bar to come down too quickly. A towel slung around the neck can act as an effective pad.

11 *Two-hand press:* This is an Olympic lift. Hold the bar across the chest about level with the shoulders as shown on the right. Press the bar slowly and evenly upwards until the arms are fully extended (locked), with the body and head held erect. Pause and lower to the chest position. Try to avoid back and knee bending when starting the press. The load thrown on the triceps, pectorals and deltoids varies slightly according to the hand position and it is a good idea to alternate between a wide and a narrow grasp during training sessions.

12 *Alternate press:* Stand astride with the arms upwards bent, dumb-bells at shoulder height. Punch the arms alternately upwards to stretch height.

The abdominal muscles form the front wall of a bowl-shaped cavity containing the intestines. This front wall is composed of three layers of muscles: the rectus abdominis; the external and internal obliques; the transversalis.

When these muscles lose their tone and sag, the intestines slip forward throwing their full weight on to the weakened muscular wall. The additional weight causes the muscles to sag even further and this in its turn allows the abdominal contents to slip further outwards still and to lie even more heavily against the muscle wall.

A sagging stomach is a sign of age and lack of exercise. Once the muscles have become stretched it is difficult to strengthen and shorten them again. The weight trainer who develops a washboard effect on his mid section is laying down the foundation for a youthful and sprightly figure in later life as well as taking out an insurance policy against digestive disorders which frequently accompany the 'protruding pot'.

The following exercises have been specially selected as being most effective in developing abdominal strength and rehabilitating weakened muscles. For the latter purpose the back lying exercises with double leg raising should be omitted as these throw too big a strain on weakened abdominals working in a lengthened condition. Exercises within the inner range, such as the trunk curls, are most suitable for those fighting the battle of the bulge.

1 *Trunk curls:* Lie on your back with your feet anchored beneath a barbell or heavy piece of furniture. Hold the hands by the side and the head and shoulders off the ground until you can just see your ankles—this is the starting position. From here lift and curl the trunk upwards until the body is almost upright. Lower down to the starting position but remember to keep head and shoulders off the ground throughout all the repetitions. A disc may be held behind the head in the later stages of training. Look at the illustration on page 37, and note how small is the range of movement; but the abdominals are working the whole time, either in a shortening action to raise the trunk forward or in a shortened static contraction to maintain the head and shoulders clear of the ground (see also page 74).

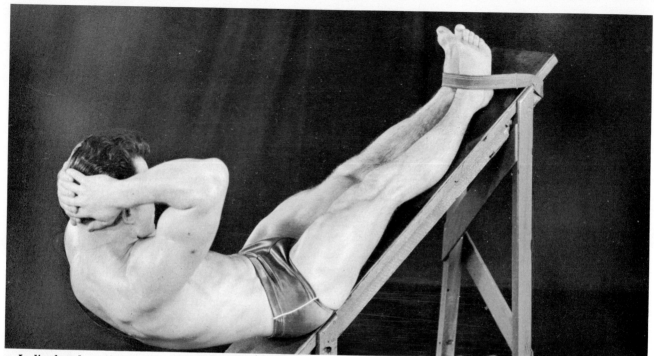

2 *Inclined curls or sit-ups:* The difference between a 'curl' and a 'sit-up' is that in the former the body is curled by the abdominals and the back is rounded whereas in the 'sit-up' the back is kept straight and the prime movers in the exercise are the hip flexor muscles. The abdominals work statically in their natural length. Lie on an inclined bench with the feet towards the raised end and tucked under a strap (a weight can be held behind neck). Either curl upwards to press the head close to the knees or sit up with a straight back to form a right angle at the hips. The curl is the more effective true abdominal exercise of the two. In this exercise, too, maximum effect can be gained by keeping

38

the head and shoulders clear for the complete set of repetitions. Rest in between each set. The greater the slope the harder the work (see page 38).

3 *Inclined sit-ups or curls with a twist:* Link hands behind head. Raise trunk, at the same time twist to reach beyond the outside of opposite knee with elbow, as shown above.

4 *Head and knee raising:* Back lying wearing iron boots, clasp the hands behind the neck. Raise the head and trunk to try to touch the knees with the elbows.

5 *'V' sitting, knee bending:* Sit in the V position, legs raised to forty-five degrees, trunk slightly leaning backwards, wearing shoes or iron boots. Bend the knees to the chest and

straighten to the starting position. Maintain your balance by sliding the tips of the fingers along the floor. Try with single knee bending, as on page 75.

6 *Leg lifting:* Lie flat on the back wearing iron boots. Raise both legs midway upwards and lower down until the heels are almost touching the ground. Don't allow the abdominals to relax by resting the heels on the ground until all the repetitions are finished.

7 *Leg lifting and crossing over:* Back lying, wearing an iron boot, arms sideways in line with the shoulders, raise leg and cross it over to touch the opposite hand (see page 73). Return to the starting position.

8 *Double leg lift and cross over:* Lie as in the previous exercise but raise both legs together, cross over until they approach the opposite hand. This is a good exercise for the oblique abdominal muscles used in throwing events and in retaining the abdominal viscera in position.

9 *Head and knee raising:* Back lying, wearing iron boots, hands clasped behind the head. Raise the head and trunk and bend the knee so as to touch the opposite knee with the elbow. Lie back and raise the other knee to be touched with the opposite elbow.

10 *Abdominal retraction:* This is the only exercise for developing the one muscle which all the other exercises have not yet touched—the transversalis—the broad sheet of muscle passing horizontally across the stomach keeping the contents in place. By retracting the stomach or pulling in the wall as far back towards the spine as possible the transversalis works against the weight of the viscera as it squeezes them into as small a space as possible. Abdominal retraction takes a little time to learn but it should be practised until a retraction similar to the one shown on page 171 can be achieved. It is an exercise which can be done at odd times of the day whenever the thought occurs.

It is in the mid section that a man first begins to show his age—when the tide comes in it comes in fast. The warning sign of the loosening of the top button of the trousers after a meal should not be ignored. It is time to exercise and to watch the diet. Even with the younger body builder, diet must be watched carefully, for remember that a well-developed set of abdominal muscles can soon be hidden by a smooth layer of fat which fills in the ridges defining the vertical and horizontal fascia of the muscles.

THE LEG MUSCLES—THE THIGH

Of all the muscles of the body, those of the thigh are perhaps the easiest to develop. They respond readily to exercise. Whenever weights are carried and the legs slightly bent it is the muscles of the thigh which work to prevent the knees from buckling under the combined poundage of the barbell and of the torso. But special exercises are needed to achieve symmetrical development and clear-cut definition.

The muscle which seems to escape most of the burden of everyday work is the vastus medialis—that strip of muscle running along the inside of the knee. You can feel it if you place your hand slightly above and to the inside of the knee as you straighten the leg against some resistance. It is the muscle which wastes so rapidly whenever the knee is injured. Exercises causing the quadriceps to work strongly against resistance during the last fifteen degrees of extension are the best ones for this muscle.

The selection of exercises given below cover all aspects of leg development and should be brought into the training schedule at varying intervals to ensure that the leg is given a thorough developmental routine.

The squat, although one of the most important and effective of all weight training exercises, should be supplemented by a wide variety of other leg exercises.

MAINLY FOR THE KNEE EXTENSORS

1 *Half squats:* The half squat is favoured by many weight trainers because a heavier weight can be handled if the knees are not fully bent on lowering the weight down. A bench or a chair can be used to indicate the lowest point in the knee bend and it ensures that the weight is lowered the same distance on each knee flexion.

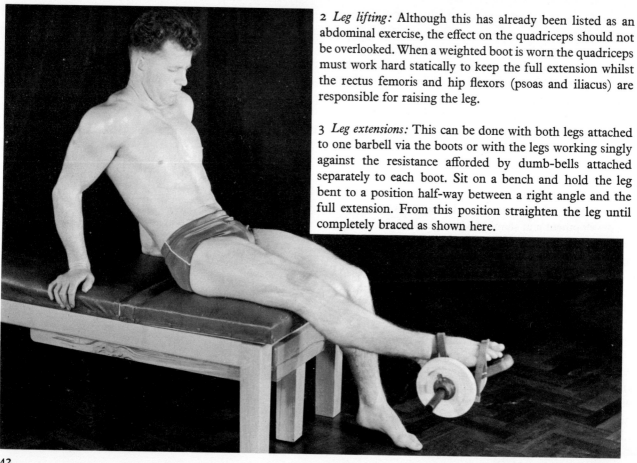

2 *Leg lifting:* Although this has already been listed as an abdominal exercise, the effect on the quadriceps should not be overlooked. When a weighted boot is worn the quadriceps must work hard statically to keep the full extension whilst the rectus femoris and hip flexors (psoas and iliacus) are responsible for raising the leg.

3 *Leg extensions:* This can be done with both legs attached to one barbell via the boots or with the legs working singly against the resistance afforded by dumb-bells attached separately to each boot. Sit on a bench and hold the leg bent to a position half-way between a right angle and the full extension. From this position straighten the leg until completely braced as shown here.

4 *Leg abduction:* Lie on one side of the body with one leg resting on top of the other. Raise the leg slowly as high as possible and lower down.

5 *Squat jumps:* Hold a lightly loaded barbell behind the neck and drop into a full knee bend with one foot in front of the other. Spring upwards to straighten the legs and whilst the feet are in the air change their positions so as to land with the opposite foot in front of the other. Pad the bar to avoid bruising. Medicine balls may be used, as shown on page 123.

6 *Hack lift:* Hold the bar behind the legs with the knuckles towards the front, hands shoulder width apart (see left). Slowly bend into a full squat position and straighten up again. The hack lift throws a greater load on the quadriceps muscles than does the squat which can shunt some of the work on to the gluteals when the body leans forwards at the hips during the squatting movement.

Even heavier weights still may be used to place resistance against the quadriceps muscles in extending the knee if a hack lift machine is used. The photograph on the right of the page shows a simple home-made machine.

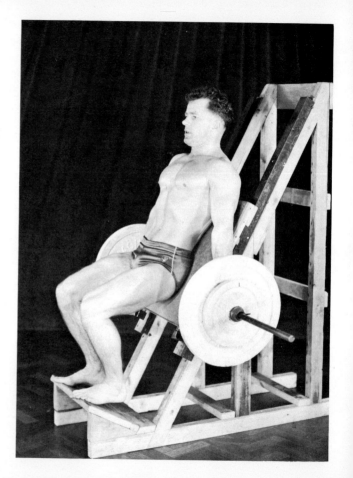

7 *Straddle lift:* This type of knee bending exercise allows the back to be kept more or less vertical. Stand astride the bar as shown on the left, with one hand in front of the legs and the other to the rear, palms facing each other. Bend and stretch the knees. Change the hand positions after each set.

8 *Single leg squat:* This is a difficult exercise even without weights. But the man with powerful thighs can do it holding a dumb-bell. In the early stages one hand can be used to steady the balance, as shown here. Stretch and bend the knee and then change hands and legs.

9 *Lunging:* Stand with the barbell resting on a pad behind the neck. Step forward a full pace bending the leading knee until the body and rear leg form a straight line (see right). Push back to the starting position.

FOR THE KNEE FLEXORS

1 *Leg curls, lying:* Lie face downwards on a bench with a weighted boot on one leg. Bend the knee backwards keeping the knee and upper thigh firmly placed on the bench. Lower slowly to the fully extended position again. The hamstrings work strongly concentrically in raising and eccentrically in lowering in this exercise.

2 *Leg curls:* Stand facing a wall with one hand used to maintain balance. Raise the booted foot until the heel approaches the back of the thigh. Lower slowly down.

FOR THE LOWER LEG

The main muscles to be developed here are those at the rear of the calf which are used when standing on tiptoe, and those running along the front and side of the shin. For the calf muscles the most effective exercises are those involving heel raising with the knees straight whilst carrying a weight across the shoulders or hips. For the more advanced weight trainer there is the calf machine (see page 14).

1 *Calf raise:* Hold a heavily weighted barbell behind the neck. Raise as high as you can on your toes to maintain a good balance throughout the movement (see right and page 72).

2 *Single heel raise from step:* Stand on the edge of a firm box or step, the free hand lightly touching the wall for support, the other hand carrying a heavy dumb-bell. Only the ball of the foot should be on the step whilst the heel should drop below the level of the toes. The calf muscles are then working from a stretched condition to raise the heel as high as possible.

3 *Donkey lift:* Stand with the body bent forward forming a right angle at the hips. Have a training partner sit on your hips. Again, using the hands to steady the balance, raise the heels as high as you can.

4 *Ankle dorsi-flexion:* For the muscles to the side and front of the shin there are not many good exercises. A resisted dorsi-flexion is what is needed most, and for this short range of movement a spring type of resistance on an iron boot modified so that a weight can be attached to the extension piece, as shown on the right, is the only satisfactory way to apply a progressive resistance to the exercise.

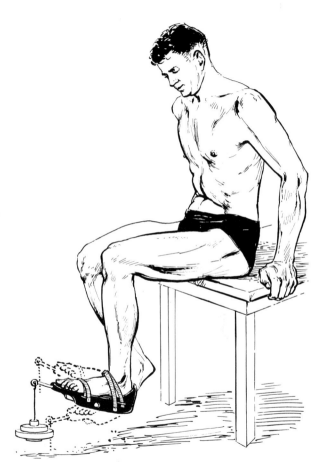

Most of us work every day with the back slightly bent forward—we may lean over a desk, work at a bench or sit in a car. Consequently the muscles of the back are continually working in a lengthened condition in order to maintain the body's equilibrium. Systematic strengthening exercises for the back muscles can compensate for this continual stooping and develop a back strong enough to avoid fatigue and strains that are incurred by those with poorer musculature.

The back muscles respond well to weight training but it is important to remember this one basic principle—never lift weights with the back bent forward and rounded. It is from such a movement that intervertebral disc trouble springs. The short muscles and ligaments retaining the discs in position between the vertebrae are easily damaged when heavy weights are lifted in this rounded back posture. Once this happens there is always the likelihood of recurring trouble.

Therefore it cannot be emphasised too much at this stage —keep the back straight when lifting. The exercises given below are those which work the dorsal muscles either in their normal length or from normal to a shortened one.

1 *Trunk raising backwards with barbell:* Lie on the bench with the feet tucked beneath a strap. Hold the barbell behind the neck and across the shoulders. Raise the trunk backwards as far as possible keeping the chin tucked in.

2 *Trunk and arms raising backwards:* Lie on a bench with arms sideways, a dumb-bell in each hand. Raise the trunk and arms backwards at the same time. Brace the shoulder blades as close together as possible (see page 51). It is easier if the feet are anchored firmly beneath a strap on the bench but keep the hips flat on the bench throughout the movement, otherwise the dorsal muscles will 'cheat' and the bulk of the work will be thrown on to the gluteals. Perform the exercise rhythmically in a 'flying' movement. Care should be taken to protect the floor or the bench from the impact of the dumb-bells which will come down with a crash from the raised position as the arms begin to tire (see also page 80).

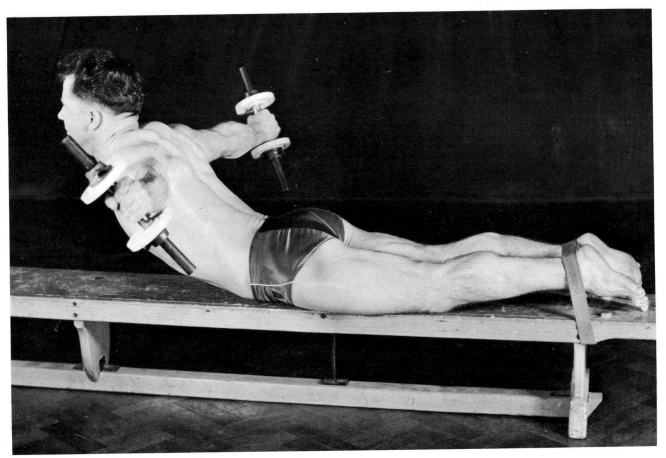

3 *Chinning, wide overgrasp:* Grasp the chinning bar as wide as possible with the palms of the hands facing the front. Heave your body upwards until the chin is level with the bar. The wide grasp with the elbows pressed back brings the latissimus dorsi forcibly into operation (see page 20).

4 *Chinning behind the neck:* Take a similar grip for this exercise and heave upwards until the bar is behind the neck, as on page 20.

5 *Single arm raising sideways and backwards:* Lean forward with one foot about half a pace in front of the other. Place the free hand on the forward knee. Raise the dumb-bell sideways as far as possible keeping the hips firm, and without turning at the waist. The weight should be raised slowly and lowered steadily.

6 *Dumb-bell rowing:* Lean forward at the waist in the same position as for the previous exercise. Hold the dumb-bell in the free hand. Bend and stretch the arm to bring the weight rhythmically to the shoulder in a rowing motion and back to the starting position again. Use a heavy dumb-bell but keep the strain from the back muscles by supporting the trunk firmly on the straight arm resting on the forward leg or bench (see right).

7 *Trunk bending sideways:* Hold a barbell behind the neck, hands placed as wide apart as possible, feet astride. Keeping the body erect bend sideways at the hips rhythmically to the left and then to the right. Do not load the bar too heavily in this exercise for the muscular effort involved is not only that needed to pull the weight over to the side but also that needed to check the momentum and gravitational pull so as to change the swing to the opposite direction. Violent swinging with a heavily loaded barbell can injure the spinal muscles (see also page 72).

What is it that gives the wedge-shaped massiveness to the well-developed chest? The bulky shoulders are formed mainly by the deltoids, the depth by the pectorals, and the width by the latissimus dorsi running down the sides of the chest wall to the rear of the ribs and on to the attachments of the spine. The fullness and added contours are provided by the finger-like striations of the serratus magnus appearing on the front and side of the lower ribs.

Building a big chest is a matter of exercising these muscles against increasing resistance and in providing such exercise that will cause a deeper and increased rate of respiration. The mobility of the chest wall will be improved and the vital capacity of the lungs increased to cope with the additional load thrown on the breathing system. Running, stepping, straddle and squat jumps are all good exercises for stimulating the respiratory system into increased activity.

The exercises described below are designed to work the muscles of the chest against an increasing load and to promote deep respiration.

1 *Straight arm pullovers:* Lie on your back on a bench with the barbell held at arm's length overhead as shown on page 55. Slowly lower the bar backwards over the head until the weights are close to the floor at arm's length behind the head. During the lowering the 'fanning' out of the rib cage will be felt as the weight reaches the end position. Raise the bar in the same path on the return movement keeping the arms straight and the hips firm on the bench. This is a first-class mobilising as well as a strengthening exercise (see also page 79).

2 *Single arm pullovers:* By using the single arm pullover you can be sure that each arm is working to capacity and not being carried by the other. Perform the exercise in the same way as for the double arm pullover.

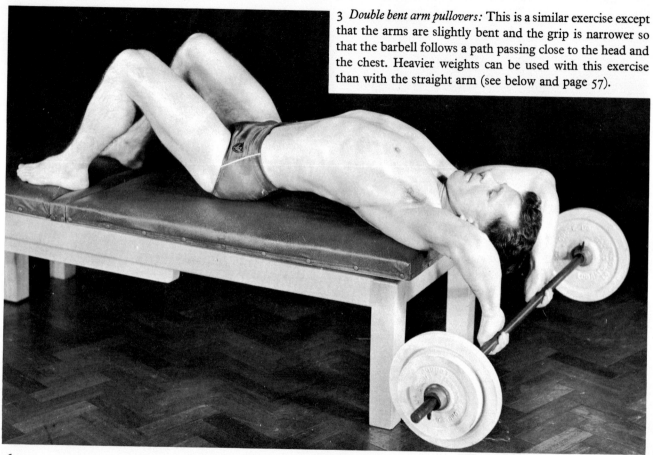

3 *Double bent arm pullovers:* This is a similar exercise except that the arms are slightly bent and the grip is narrower so that the barbell follows a path passing close to the head and the chest. Heavier weights can be used with this exercise than with the straight arm (see below and page 57).

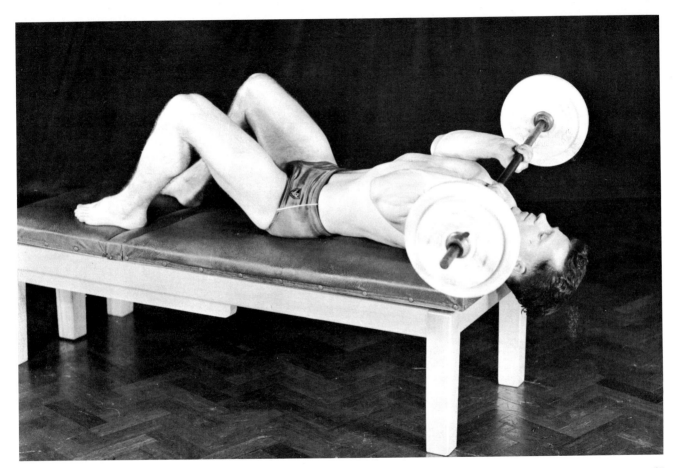

4 *Bench press* (*barbell*): Lie on the bench holding the barbell across the chest, wide grasp. Press the weight upwards to stretch height above the shoulders, keeping the arms vertical. If the hands are close together, more work is done by the triceps and less by the pectorals (see above and page 59).

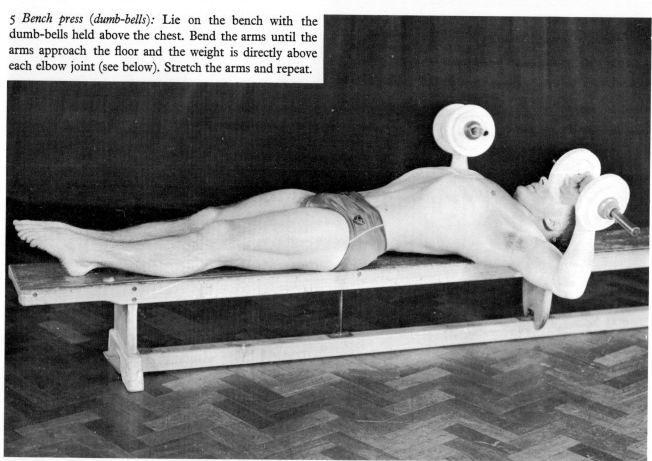

5 *Bench press* (*dumb-bells*): Lie on the bench with the dumb-bells held above the chest. Bend the arms until the arms approach the floor and the weight is directly above each elbow joint (see below). Stretch the arms and repeat.

6 *Bent arm raise, lying:* Lie on your back with the arms sideways and slightly bent at the elbow. Hold the dumbbells with the thumbs uppermost. Raise the weights to the stretch position above the chest and lower slowly down. By changing the hand position so that the thumbs are towards the ground different fibres of the pectorals and deltoids can be exercised (see page 78).

EXERCISES FOR GENERAL ENDURANCE

General organic endurance is the ability to withstand long periods of exhausting muscular activity and to delay the effects of fatigue. It is not merely a physical condition for it depends also upon indefinable factors such as will-power, motivation, faith, morale and the ability to override the symptoms of fatigue and so carry on when the failing body indicates that it has had enough. But all other things being equal, the man with the well-trained circulatory and respiratory system is the one most likely to postpone the onset of fatigue and its deleterious effects during strenuous physical activity and discomfort.

Exercise has been described as the flywheel which sets in motion all the other functions of the body. Energy is burnt and so the muscles call for more oxygen and fuel. This is carried by the blood to the active muscles. The lungs work harder to supply the oxygen and the heart pumps more quickly and strongly to drive the oxygen-laden blood to the active muscles. When the exercise is finished the digestive system is more active to replenish the stocks of easily assimilated foodstuffs to be used as fuel for energy.

The heart and respiratory muscles, although different in structure to the skeletal muscles, respond to progressive resistance exercises in the same way—they become bigger and stronger. Running is one of the best exercises for the development of general organic efficiency and endurance but it is not always easy for town-dwellers to find the time or conditions suitable for long distance running and so they must make use of weight training exercises which strenuously work the large muscle groups of the legs. Remember that the leg muscles comprise nearly two-thirds of the total muscle mass of the body and when they are exercised they make big demands on the circulatory and respiratory systems. The circuit training exercises described on pages 119 to 142 are recommended.

5 Weight training in schools

FOR MANY years, and with gratifying results, weight training has been given to boys. Strength development has been more rapid and boys have preferred the challenge provided by weight training to the conventional Scandinavian-type exercises which used to form the strengthening part of schools' physical education periods.

Even boys who are not normally inclined towards vigorous games are sometimes attracted to weight training. Somehow it captures their imagination. Perhaps the appeal is the satisfaction of being able to do some physical activity without failing or it may be the stimulus of self-testing. Boys always try to beat their best performance. They like making progress and in weight training this is easily seen without the teacher or coach having to point it out. Once boys begin to feel stronger, they train harder, demand more from their muscles, and develop self-confidence in their physical ability.

Despite the experience of schools where weight training has been part of the physical education curriculum and the reports of research carried out by university physical education departments, there are still many critics of weight training who oppose the use of barbells in the school gymnasium. Yet the same people appear to see little wrong in one boy struggling to carry another in a game of 'Horses and Jockeys' or 'Fireman's lift' relay, where there is a far greater risk of injury, through staggering about off balance and perhaps being pushed whilst carrying the heavy weight of another boy. It is far safer to exercise with barbells where the weight is accurately gauged to suit each individual's ability and only moved when the performer is firmly poised in the correct position for the exercise.

Obviously there will always be some risk through boys trying to outshine one another in strength, by lifting more than they should, just as they sometimes try to jump further or swing higher in other activities. And, of course, the same careful and unobtrusive supervision is essential to protect them from their over-enthusiastic efforts.

The principle of steady progression must be instilled into young weight trainers at the very beginning and a strict code of conduct regarding simple safety precautions has to be enforced in a tactful manner that does not subdue youthful enthusiasm. All boys must thoroughly understand the safety precautions listed on page 7.

But boys, like men, want to know why there are rules and regulations. If a reason for each can be given, that is simple to understand and makes sense, then they are more likely to follow the advice, to adopt a superior attitude to those who don't and tell them what will happen if they are not more careful.

Boys will readily accept the explanation that cold muscles tear more easily than warm ones. Many will have had experience of pain through 'pulling' a muscle, and they can easily see that straining to complete one more repetition in a set may cause unnecessary damage to muscles or to the heart, but what is more difficult for them to understand is why the breath must never be held when lifting heavy weights. The phenomenon of Valsalva is not an easy one to put over.

A simplified explanation is that if, when a weight is being lifted, the breath is held by locking the glottis, like a cork holding fizzy lemonade in a bottle, the pressure inside the chest cavity increases enormously and forces the blood from the lungs' blood vessels into the arteries together with the flow of blood pumped from the heart. This increases the total outward flow and so causes the blood pressure in the arteries to rise. At the same time, owing to this abnormally high compression in the chest cavity, the blood returning through the veins is unable to force its way back to the heart. Consequently, because the supply of blood to the heart has been restricted, the supply pumped to the arteries decreases and arterial blood pressure drops alarmingly. The pulse beat may almost disappear whilst the veins stand out like knotted cords. At this stage, with the heart compressed, thereby reducing the size of the compartment receiving returning blood, the effort of the lift may finish and the breath be explosively released. Thus, when the pressure is vented, the heart dilates and blood rushes into its chambers. This extra inflow causes the arterial pressure to jump excessively high again. Sudden changes in arterial pressure can be dangerous in people with circulatory or respiratory weaknesses and it is important that boys should not strain in lifting to such an extent that breathing is temporarily suspended. Always, breathing should be as free and natural as possible. To counteract any tendency to hold the breath when lifting, some coaches teach breathing out purposefully as the weight is raised.

The object of keeping the back straight is to avoid damage to the small intervertebral muscles and ligaments which help to keep the soft fibrous discs in position between the vertebrae. Lifting with a rounded back is one of the main causes of disc lesions. When the small intervertebral muscles tear, the disc protrudes and presses on the sciatic nerve root causing pain down the back, buttock and leg.

What risk is there of rupture or 'herniation' through weight training? Just as strain with restricted breathing sets up increased pressure within the chest, so squats with very heavy weights increase the pressure within the abdominal cavity. If there is any anatomical weakness in the abdominal wall then weight training may expose it and cause part of the intestines to protrude through a gap in the muscle fibres. The commonest site is in the lower part of the abdominal wall immediately above the inner side of the inguinal ligament. The same herniation can just as easily be caused through excessive strain in defaecation, coughing or in lifting a heavy piece of furniture.

Gradual progression is a reasonable safeguard against overstrain. It is not so much during a steady and maximal effort that the risk is greatest but when a boy loses his balance through trying to handle an excessively heavy load. In attempting to prevent the weights crashing to the floor he may place an abnormally heavy strain on muscle groups not made for such loads. Once heavy weights are used boys should work in pairs or threes so that assistance is always at hand for the beginning and end of a set of exercises.

The final precaution needs no elaboration. A 10-lb disc sliding off a bar through a loose locking nut can easily break one of the small bones of the foot causing, perhaps, years of troublesome foot pain.

Such are the main risks in weight training for boys. They are not as fearsome as the possibility of a broken neck or limbs in vaulting and agility exercises, or concussion in rugby. And if strength development is regarded as a worthwhile aim in boys' exercise programmes then the most effective methods should be used. Experience and research leave little doubt that weight training is the most rapid way of achieving that aim.

Use of equipment

One of the biggest problems facing the physical education teacher introducing weight training into the curriculum is how to make the best use of the limited amount of equipment available for a class of thirty pupils. How can he keep them all purposefully employed and interested in the lesson? Few schools have enough equipment to provide each pupil with either a barbell or dumb-bell and consequently some improvisation is usually necessary.

For some exercises using weight a barbell is not necessary—medicine balls or plastic water-containers make serviceable substitutes. Eight pints of water, for example, weigh about 14 lb.

The discs themselves can be used without the barbell to increase the difficulty of an exercise. For instance, a 10-lb disc held in both hands behind the neck in the prone-lying position greatly increases the resistance to be overcome by dorsal muscles in the trunk raising backwards exercise. It is also more comfortable than a barbell held against the spine.

Alternatively, a class may be put on group activities so that only a few pupils at a time are weight training. The remainder may be practising skills or tackling some form of endurance training not requiring weights.

Specialised weight training for sport

The aim of all weight training with boys should be general physical development and it would be wrong for them to aim at such an early age for specific strength needed in a particular sport. Boys should be exposed to as many sports and physical recreations as possible before they begin to specialise. Let them first develop a burning desire to become the best at one sport before training becomes specific and directed. The desire to play, to win and to train must come from within the boy himself. There is always a temptation for fathers and coaches to lead a boy into a preferred sport but it is better to let the boy make up his own mind after trying his hand at many activities.

Medical opinion on weight training for boys

Typical of the current trend of medical opinion is that expressed by Dr Roswell Gallagher, M.D., who writes convincingly of the value of weight training for young people. He argues that boys and youths are bound to play together in their leisure time. The younger ones will strive to emulate the prowess of their elder brothers in games and in doing so are likely to suffer from over-fatigue and possible strains of the ankle, knee and lower back. If they are going to play together, the younger ones should be built up first to take the strain of competition with those of more mature development. It is no good telling a boy that he is too young to play or to take it easy because, as soon as he sees a game begin, he will be in it and playing as though his life depended on the result. Dr Roswell Gallagher believes that carefully supervised weight training exercises would strengthen the muscles supporting weaker joints and so render them less susceptible to injury. Once a ligament is damaged it heals with scar tissue which is never quite the same. It is not as strong and is less elastic.

A lot of good work has been done with weight training in the rehabilitation of injuries but it is probably true to say that many of the injured would never have been needing rehabilitation if they had been adequately strengthened before participating in vigorous and violent games. Rather than causing injury, weight training for boys and youths can be a preventive.

There can, after all, be only two kinds of exercise—objective or incidental. Objective exercise aims through deliberate movements to achieve improvements of muscular strength, power, mobility, endurance and skill, whereas incidental exercise is that derived whilst enjoying the playing of a game or in the performance of some physical activity. Now if strengthening is to be regarded as a worthwhile aim in boys' exercise programmes, then the most efficient and carefully graded exercises should be used to achieve that aim.

An ideal machine for strengthening the leg muscles of rowers is here demonstrated by Manfred Rulffs of the 'BRC-Welle-Poseidon'.

Very heavy weights can be used without the risk of injury which could occur through faulty handling of conventional barbells. From this point of view it is an ideal machine for boys and girls wishing to use heavy weights.

An interesting feature is that the machine can be adapted to provide for variations in the angle of thrust from the legs.

Boys of King's School, Gütersloh, basketball team with light weights used in a training circuit to develop stamina.

Ideally boys should work in pairs so that one is always ready to assist his partner to adopt the starting position and to lower the weights to the floor after the exercise is finished. This minimises the risk of injury.

6 Weight training for women and girls

THERE HAVE been heated arguments about the effects of vigorous exercise on women ever since they first competed in the Olympic Games more than forty years ago. Many physical education specialists say that women should not copy men in their sports but should devise and develop sports more suitable to the frailer frame of women.

On the other hand, little evidence has been produced to show that athletics and sport adversely affect women. In fact, medical opinion seems to be summed up by Sir Arthur Porritt, Governor-General of New Zealand, formerly Sergeant Surgeon to Her Majesty The Queen, who, writing in *Modern Athletics*,[1] says: 'Structurally it has been amply proved that a woman's frame is just as adequate as a man's.' What is clear, however, is that if women do compete in sports requiring strength and stamina then they need to develop these qualities in training.

The remarkable progress that has been made in women's athletic and sports performance in recent years has called for a high degree of dedication and self-discipline. To succeed now, it is not enough to have a natural aptitude for sports. Time must be spent not only in mastering techniques but also in acquiring the strength and stamina to use these techniques under the stress of top-class competition.

Initially women have a relatively lower level of muscular strength than men. They therefore have a greater need for specific training. This demands time. But enough time for training is always difficult to find.

The young have a wide variety of social and recreational demands on their leisure time whilst those who are older often have responsibilities which curtail their recreational activities even more.

Obviously it is important that every training session should produce a worthwhile effect. Haphazard training is a waste of time and effort. Without much doubt the way to develop stamina and strength in women is the way used so successfully by men; namely, through weight training, isometric exercise and circuit training. There is nothing revolutionary in women and girls using weights. Miss M. T. Crabbe, Principal of the I. M. Marsh College of Physical Education, reported that girls in boarding schools were training with weights and Indian clubs in the late nineteenth century.[2] Fashion models and film stars with little time to spare for sport have been using dumb-bells for many years to keep their figures trim. When planning a training schedule there can be no place for vague objections to weight training based more on prejudice than physiological fact.

Enjoy exercising with light weights at first and remember, when you exercise with enthusiasm you get fit quickly.

Types of exercise

Weight training exercises which have proved effective for men are nearly all suitable for women, provided that adjustments are made to poundage and repetitions according to each individual's ability. Movement by movement, there is little difference between a man's performance and that of a woman in the same athletic event. The mechanics of the muscle action in putting the shot, for example, are the same for a man as for a woman.

It seems sensible then for women to employ training methods which have been successful in improving the men's ability.

Frequently with women, inadequate strength and insufficient powers of endurance are the fundamental causes of poor style. Time is often wasted in practising a technique which is too difficult for the muscles to perform correctly. A good coach can best decide how the time available for training should be most usefully apportioned to developing the six basic attributes of good performance: strength, endurance, skill, speed, agility and motivation.

Physiological considerations

The principle of overload or progressive resistance applies equally to female and male muscles: both develop through being made to work against a resistance which increases progressively as the muscle develops. There need be no fear of strain or excessive development of muscle bulk if the training programme is carefully graded to each individual's ability.

Medical opinion

Medical opinion is still divided on the question of whether girls in puberty should take part in highly competitive sport or vigorous exercise, but it is safe to say that if training is coupled progressively with competition, sport or athletics can become a source of physical, social and psychological benefit. Weight training is a sure way of doing this without placing undue strain on the performer.

Menstruation, pregnancy and motherhood

Most women tend to restrict physical activity during menstruation, yet research has shown that there appears to be no need for this. Naturally, there is bound to be a good deal of variation from one individual to the next, and although menstruation itself may make little difference to physical potentiality the psychological effect plus the temporary additional fluid retention in the body might result in some diminution in performance.

Pregnancy, in the early weeks, appears to have no adverse effect on athletic performance. Research[3] into the effects of exercise on motherhood indicates that even at the level of world-class competition physical exercise has a beneficial effect on motherhood.

When the obstetric histories of outstanding women athletes were carefully studied by Dr Pfeifer[4] it was evident that the duration of labour was shorter with the athlete than with the sedentary woman and the fertility ratios were about the same. There appears to be no factual evidence to support the argument, sometimes heard, that violent exercise is harmful to motherhood. In fact, the evidence points to the opposite conclusion.

Exercises for women

The following pages show some exercises that are particularly recommended for women and girls.

REFERENCES

1 Sir Arthur Porritt, Bt., G.C.M.G., K.C.V.O., K.B.E., M.Ch. (Oxon), F.R.C.S., 'Medical Science and the Future', *Modern Athletics* (Achilles Club).

2 'The Place of Gymnastics in Education', report to the *Third International Congress on Physical Education and Sport for Girls and Women*, 1957.

3 Sir Adolphe Abrahams, O.B.E., M.D., F.R.C.P., 'Medical Aspects of Physical Exercise', *Triangle*, Vol. III, No. 8.

4 W. A. Pfeifer, 'Sportlicher Wettkampf und Geburtsverlauf' *Sport und Leiberziehung* (Enke-Verlag, Stuttgart).

EXERCISES FOR WOMEN

1 Stand with front part of foot raised on a block of wood or a thick book, lower the heel and raise it rhythmically to develop the calf muscles. Increase the weight of the dumbbell held to increase the severity of the exercise.

2 *Calf raise:* Exercise for lower leg development (see page 48).

3 *Trunk bending sideways:* Starting position for this dorsal exercise (see page 53).

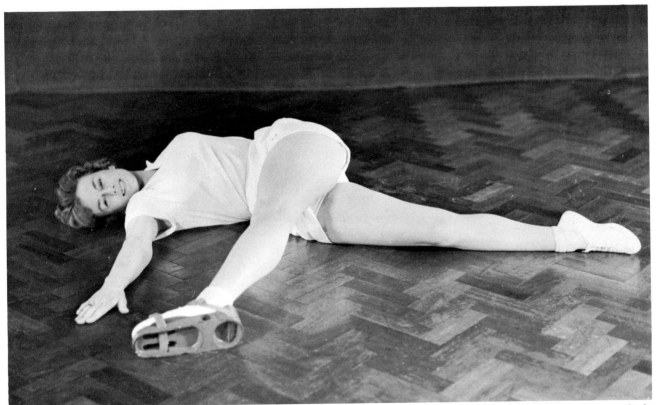

4 *Leg lifting and crossing over:* Wearing an iron boot this is a good exercise for the oblique abdominal muscles. It is described on page 40. Try to keep the shoulders flat on the ground throughout the movement and control the leg lowering down.

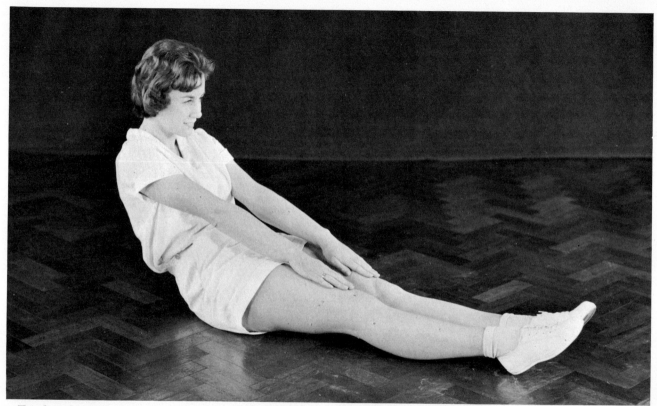

5 *Trunk curls:* One of the most effective of all abdominal exercises. Note in the final position shown here the body is not upright. The abdominal muscles are therefore tensed, not relaxed as they would be in the upright position (see page 36 for full description).

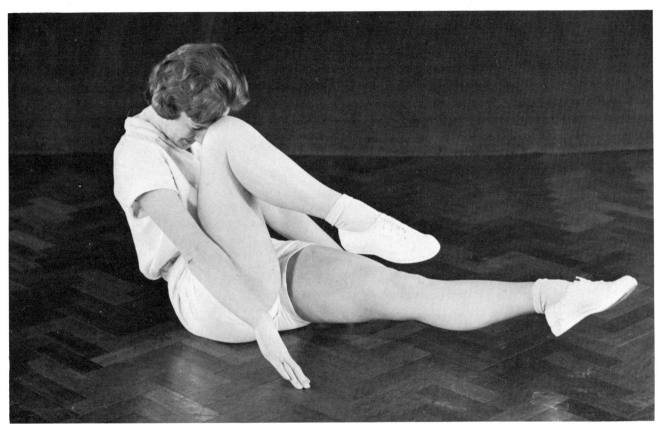

6 '*V*' *sitting, single knee bending:* This is a strong abdominal exercise which is not as difficult as it looks. Maintain the balance by sliding the fingertips forward as the knee is lifted (see page 39 for full description).

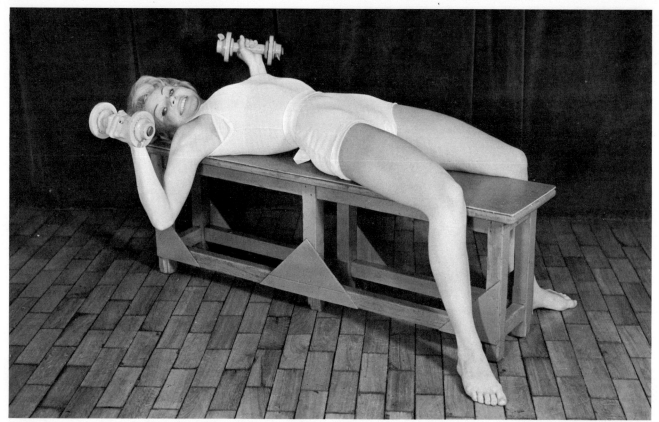

7 Bench press: With dumb-bells held above the elbow joints (as above) raise the arms to stretch position above the chest (see page 77). This exercise develops the pectoral and triceps muscles (see also page 60).

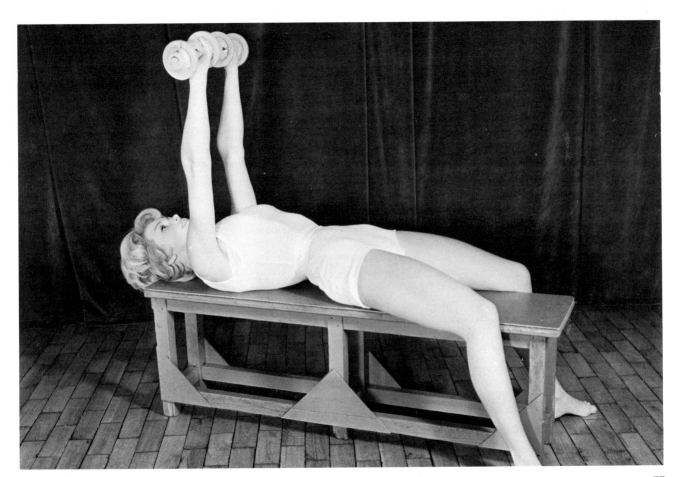

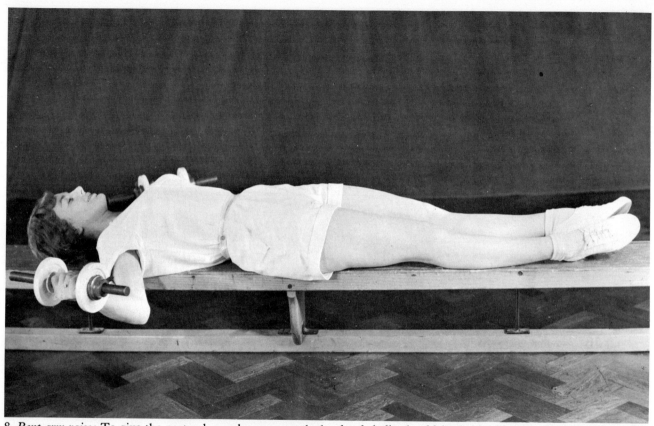

8 *Bent arm raise:* To give the pectoral muscles more work the dumb-bells should be held wider apart (see also page 61).

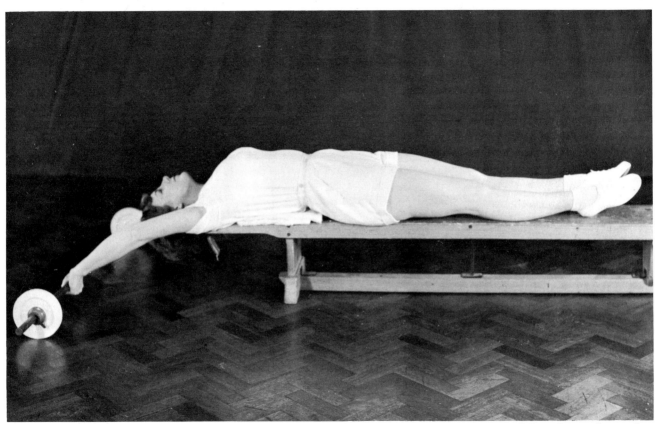

9 *Straight arm pullovers:* This exercise, which is described on page 54, develops the chest muscles and also helps to maintain thoracic mobility. Use a very light weight at first so that full control can be maintained when the barbell is lowered.

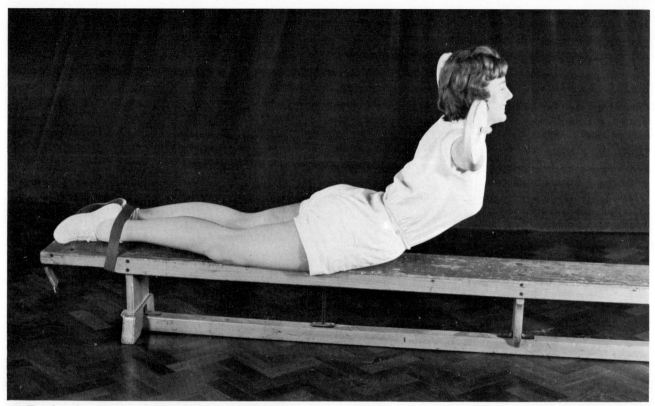

10 *Trunk and arms raising backwards:* Disc weights are used here instead of dumb-bells which would be too heavy for most women.

Note how the arms are pressed well back and the weights held in line with the shoulders (see page 50 for full description).

11 A disc weight can be tied with tape to the foot to provide extra weight in exercises for the thigh muscles. Increase the weight gradually. Iron boots may be used if available (see page 42).

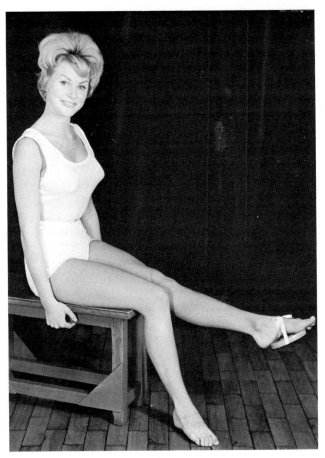

Girls of King's School, Gütersloh. In one corner of the gym there is ample room for half a dozen girls to train.

How young to start? In his book, 'Strength Training for Athletics', Ron Pickering, chief coach to the Amateur Athletic Association, says, 'Opinions differ on how young one should begin strength training but it is more generally accepted for boys and girls who are past puberty.'

Here, two pupils are demonstrating seated arm curls and the single arm press. You should begin with light weights and gradually increase the poundage as skill and strength increase. The girl preparing for a single arm press would have a firmer base if her feet were about 12 inches apart. (See similar exercises for the elbow flexors on pages 15 to 18.)

7 Weight training for athletics

STRIKING PROGRESS has been made in athletic performances during the last twenty years. Times and distances previously believed impossible have been achieved. How can this be explained? Coaching is better organised, schools give more time to athletics, television has stimulated interest and competition is keener. Consequently training methods have become more intensive and scientific physiologists, coaches and physical education specialists have evolved effective training programmes which make maximum use of time and facilities available. And featuring prominently in all these conditioning programmes is weight training.

For events which involve the overcoming of some heavy external resistance, it is generally agreed that strength is now the dominating factor influencing performance. Whereas for events requiring prolonged repetitive contractions against a relatively light resistance, endurance is the prime factor. Experiments have shown that both strength and endurance can be built rapidly and conveniently through weight training.

Obviously no two athletes are alike and it is up to the athlete himself to assess critically his own physique, his progress, the time available for training, the ultimate goal and then plan his programme for improving strength, stamina and skill.

Training for throwing events

Each of the four main throwing events requires power generated in different ways but the performance depends principally on the transference of momentum from the body via the hand to the implement being thrown.

In throwing the javelin, momentum is gained from the running steps taken prior to the final throwing posture, then the arm is thrown back to put the throwing muscles on maximum stretch before the final impelling pull. The elastic recoil of the stretched muscles is thus utilised to assist the powerful contraction of the prime throwing muscles. The posture adopted before the throw is such that the whole body untwists itself in one explosive effort bringing into play the leg extensor and trunk rotator muscles. The final power imparted to the javelin is therefore a cumulative one derived from nearly all the major muscle groups of the body.

It requires precise neuro-muscular efficiency to co-ordinate the forces as they pass from one segment of the body to the next; from the legs to the hips, trunk, arm, wrist and fingers. The successful javelin thrower is the man who makes the best use of all these forces. If his strength is great and co-ordination superb, he should be in world championship class, for it is the combination of strength and speed which gives power.

The discus- and hammer-throwing techniques are restricted by the rules governing the manner of throwing. It is not possible to gain momentum from a run-up and the weight is too heavy for the arm to be flung back, to place the throwing muscles on stretch as with the javelin, in order to utilise muscular elastic recoil. Because the implements are thrown with the elbow straight, the extensors of the arm, used in other throws, cannot assist. The throwing power for the discus and hammer events therefore must come from the impetus gained from the spin turn and the rotational power of the trunk and leg muscles as the body is whipped round and upwards in the line of flight needed for the final delivery. If the arm is allowed to trail well behind, as it should in the turns with the discus, the pectorals and anterior fibres of the deltoid are kept on stretch until the final thrust when the arm is swung forward and partial use may then be made of elastic recoil to assist the muscle pulling the arm forward.

Again, due to the restriction of the throwing circles, great skill and practice is necessary, first of all to build up such force and then to control and unleash it from within the circle and in the right direction.

Finally, with the 16-lb shot the weight is so heavy and difficult to handle that spin techniques are not possible.

86

There is therefore little space in which to overcome inertia and to gain momentum so as to release additional explosive power into the final thrust.

The aim of all training for throwing events should be to build all-round physical strength and stamina, to develop the technique of increasing speed in the momentum-gaining steps, and to perfect the exact neuro-muscular co-ordination to control and release the power within the confines of the throwing area. These are the factors to be considered by athletes planning a training programme. Progress in strength should go hand-in-hand with increases in speed and improvement in technique. A balanced programme achieving steady progress in each of these main factors is essential to optimum final achievement.

FAULTY STYLE CAN NEUTRALISE STRENGTH

Faults in style can dissipate the resources of strength built over months of assiduous weight training. If the final throwing stance is poor, the throwing action will be impeded and so lessen the power of delivery. If the feet are not firmly placed on the ground or if the surface is slippery, power is lost because one of the feet slides backwards at the moment of thrust. Attention must be paid to detail if the best results are to be obtained from great strength.

FACTORS AFFECTING PERFORMANCE

To sum up, performance in throwing events depends upon:

1 Building up body momentum and the smooth summation of the forces imparted by each segment of the body.

2 The accurate co-ordination of strength and speed to give maximum impelling power.

3 The trajectory of the delivery. The optimum angle is about forty degrees except for the discus where, owing to the aerodynamic lift, the angle of release should be a little lower—about thirty-five degrees.

4 Skill in directing all the forces along the given line of flight with minimum loss through faults in style.

5 Stamina to maintain a high degree of skill and to delay the onset of fatigue.

6 The footing and posture for the final delivery. The aim of training must then be the development of strength, stamina, speed, skill and co-ordination. The greater the strength, the greater the skill required to use it.

SUGGESTIONS FOR ROUTINES FOR THROWING EVENTS

During the winter conditioning programme, weight training should aim at all-round strength. Specific exercises can be introduced for muscle groups more immediately concerned with the final effort. The following table is given as suitable for all throwers and additional exercises for particular events are provided after the main routine.

1 *Two-hand press* (arm and shoulder extensor exercise *11*, page 35).
2 *Trunk raising backwards* (dorsal exercise *1*, page 50).
3 *Inclined sit-ups with twist* (abdominal exercise *3*, page 39).
4 *Squat jumps* (knee extensor exercise *5*, page 43).
5 *Bench press* (chest exercise *4*, page 58).
6 *Leg lifting and crossing over* (abdominal exercise *7*, page 40).
7 *Calf raise* (lower leg exercise *1*, page 48).

The exercises should be done in heavy sets permitting only a few repetitions in each set.

Favourite exercises which international athletes have used extensively and found beneficial are:

FOR THE SHOT

Shoulder shrugging from back lying: Lie on your back with a heavy barbell held at stretch height above the shoulders so that the arms are perpendicular to the ground. Push or shrug the shoulders forward keeping the arms straight throughout. This develops the serratus anterior muscle which pulls the scapula forward during the putting action. As the movement is over a very short range the maximum weight possible should be used.

FOR THE DISCUS

Bent arm raise, lying (chest exercise 6, page 61): This is a favourite exercise among discus throwers for it develops great strength in the pectorals and anterior fibres of the deltoids. The best effects are gained when the exercise is done from a bench high enough to allow the arms to fall back as far as possible before they touch the ground. These muscles are then worked from a stretched position. If the elbows are bent slightly then a greater weight can be handled.

FOR THE HAMMER

Trunk and arms raising backwards (dorsal exercise 2, page 50): This exercise is strongly recommended for developing the rear fibres of the deltoid as well as the rhomboids and other dorsal muscles used in the final delivery of the hammer throw.

Running events

It is easy to understand that strong muscles are needed for such events as putting the shot, but not all athletes would readily agree that strength is essential in running too. They would speak of inherent natural speed, say that sprinters were born and not made, and assert that running endurance can be best achieved by running on the track, road, or cross-country.

Up to a point they are right. Running will develop endurance and the cross-country event is used by many of the track men as a winter conditioning programme, but endurance does not affect speed and essentially the man who wins is the man who runs the distance in the shortest possible time; speed is the yardstick of success, speed over the given distance. To have speed there must be power and the basis of power is strength.

Perhaps the easiest way to picture the muscle power needed in running is to think of the action of a runner's legs as seen on a slow-motion film. In this way the forward motion is shown to be comprised of a series of propulsive thrusts initiated by the rear leg as it forcibly extends against the ground. The legs are brought alternately under the body to give a moment or two of support in between each forward thrust. The rear leg is therefore projecting the body weight—say 150 to 200 lb—forwards and upwards in the same way as the arm projects the shot. The 16-lb ball is put by means of a strong contraction of the arm extensors (assisted greatly by the muscles straightening the legs and rotating the trunk) and the 150-lb body weight is propelled by the hip, knee and ankle extensors of one leg. It takes a high degree of strength to make these propelling movements in quick succession.

As the speed of the runner increases, his body weight is projected forwards and upwards clear of the ground for a greater distance and period of time until eventually, when top speed has been reached, the forward leg begins to swing back and bends slightly at the knee before striking the ground with the ball of the foot almost directly below the body's centre of gravity. The period of support in between each successive drive from the rear leg becomes less and less as the speed increases.

Further observation of such a slow-motion film would reveal that the runner's legs are apparently exerting a greater driving force against the ground during the first 20 to 40 yards, when the body is inclining forwards, the stride shorter and more staccato, than when maximum speed has been reached and a more erect running angle of the body adopted. The holes in the track made by the feet pushing against the cinders are evidence of the fact that the stride lengthens and the impelling thrust diminishes after the accelerating period is passed. The effort is then directed from the task of acceleration to that of moving the limbs rapidly and maintaining a long stride. The impact of the foot in doing this is less than it is during the earlier part of the race. Of course there are athletes who tend to continue needlessly with this pounding of the track after reaching top speed, but because of the inevitable shortening of stride which this fault in style produces, there is a loss of mechanical efficiency and speed. If the track were soft and muddy such a runner would be at an even greater disadvantage for he would dissipate a good deal of power and tend to roll and lose balance.

But back to the slow-motion film. It shows graphically that muscular strength is needed for two purposes. First to provide the initial power to propel 150 lb of body weight through the air and secondly to move the legs rapidly between each successive thrust. This involves a quick swing forward, check of momentum and rapid change of direction to swing back again. There should now be no doubt that considerable strength is needed. This leaves only one question to be answered.

HOW MUCH STRENGTH IS REQUIRED?

It is often said that the car with a big engine makes a better get-away than the one with a small power pack. This comparison is used to impress readers of athletics books of the need for power and muscular development but the comparison can be misleading. There is a flaw in the logic, for some high-powered cars with heavy bodies may be more sluggish in acceleration than lighter cars geared to make better use of their power, but, with certain reservations to be discussed later, it can be said of both cars and sprinters that the greater the power pack, the greater the acceleration.

The main power for the sprinter comes from the muscles of the thigh and buttock but there is an important ancillary thrust, coming from the strong contraction of the calf muscles, which extends the ankle. The final vigorous push from the ankle increases the length of stride which in itself helps to increase the speed.

Many sprinters have been photographed doing arm curls and presses with dumb-bells, yet the function of the arm movements in running are vastly different from those of the legs and it is debatable whether such strength is essential for the arms. There is no external resistance to be overcome by the arms in running. The legs push against the ground, the arms against the air and the alternating rotary movements of the body. Percy Cerutty, world-famous athletics coach, argues differently. He advises heavy weight training routines to develop strong arm and shoulder muscles.

The arm punches across the body to prevent the shoulders swinging in the same direction as the hips and causing an inefficient rolling action. The arms must work against the resistance of the other muscles in the body and there is no doubt that the type of arm movement has a great effect on style and length of stride. Strong back, shoulder and neck muscles steady the non-moving parts of the body and provide a fixed anchorage from which work the primary muscles of running.

It is interesting to note how the running action of any athlete changes when strain and fatigue begin to tell. To the experienced eye of the coach the changes which occur give a clue to the additional training needed for improvement in technique and strength. The tired runner appears to allow his shoulders and neck to wobble, the head is often allowed to sink backwards as the eyes search the skies for help. The head, being a weighty object, has a considerable effect on body balance. When it sags backwards on to the shoulders the angle of body lean is affected and this has an adverse effect on style and mechanical efficiency. The length of stride is cut which causes the driving action of the legs to be reduced in order to prevent the athlete from falling off balance. The fatigue in one muscle group which may cause excessive tension in another again results in loss of speed. There has got to be strength for stability as well as strength for propulsion. For the legs, the accent of training should be on strength and endurance whereas for the arms and remaining muscle groups the emphasis should be more on stamina as well as strength.

There are some coaches who maintain that a runner cannot be too strong but yet they would really not advocate the development of 'Mr Universe' for a cross-country runner. Only the athlete himself can decide where to draw the line. Only he can decide, by the way he feels and the results he achieves, when he has reached his optimum strength. Then he can drop weight training and concentrate more on style, race tactics and endurance.

CAN TOO MUCH STRENGTH BE A HANDICAP?

Just to keep strength in its proper perspective, it would be as well to consider the physiological implications of excessive muscular bulk for runners because there is for them a danger in over-development. Muscles in themselves can be a retarding handicap by the resistance which they can provide against each other and within themselves.

When extensor muscles contract, the flexors must relax, or 'pay out the slack' to allow the movement to take place. For example, when the quadriceps contract and straighten the leg at the knee, the hamstrings carefully pay out enough slack to allow the full range of extension; otherwise the leg would remain partially bent. Some men, because of their occupations, as, for example, miners working continually in crouching positions, develop short hamstrings because their legs spend most of the time partly bent. If compensatory exercises are not done, the hamstrings become shorter by habit. They are not then capable of paying out the additional slack, as it were, to allow a complete extension. But even with a trained athlete, when the hamstrings do relax they retain sufficient tone to control the movement so that the knee is not pulled violently into a painful extension. This reciprocal relaxation must be considered in the training of athletes, for no matter how fine a pitch of training the muscles are in, and how well co-ordinated in relaxation and stimulation, there will always be some resistance offered by the relaxing muscles controlling the contraction. Big muscles offer more resistance in this respect than do the small. It is partly due to residual tone and partly to the elastic tension of muscle fibres, fascia and tendons.

The viscosity of a muscle is another factor providing a retarding resistance, but this can be reduced by suitable warming-up and mobilising exercises before the event.

Finally, there is the resistance within the muscle itself during contraction. A muscle contracts against its own substance: it has to compress the cells and fibres into a more compact space. The stronger the muscles, the greater the bulk to be compressed and more internal resistance has to be overcome. It can be argued that there is more power in a bigger muscle to overcome this increased internal resistance, and again the answer to the question of whether the increased power is worth the increased resistance cannot be dogmatic. So we come back again to the comparison between the acceleration of the big and the small horse-power car. The ideal power is that which is most suitable for the job to be done and the power should be geared so that maximum use is made of it. The untrained man can normally only exert about 75 per cent of his potential muscular power. Under stress of fear, anger, hypnotism or madness he can pull out some of the remaining 25 per cent. The trained man can utilise his power more efficiently; by improving his style less effort is wasted and with continued practice in certain activities he is able to utilise a greater proportion of his strength.

Training with weights for runners should be directed towards the achievement of optimum strength before the season begins and thereafter weights should be used to maintain this strength should running itself fail to keep up the required level. Apart from developing strength and stamina, pre-season weight training can help to prevent many of the early season injuries which can put back an athlete in his training programme for weeks. It is a convenient conditioner for those who have difficulty in getting out for running practice but most of all it is essential for providing the strength upon which speed and acceleration depend.

Training requirements for different events

Style, strength and stamina requirements vary according to the event. Marathon running is the most relaxed of the running styles: there is very little vigorous thrusting action to be seen in the movements of legs or arms whereas sprinting is an expression of explosive and violent effort. The sprinter has to overcome inertia in the shortest possible time and to accelerate rapidly he requires very strong muscles which respond quickly. His race may be over in ten seconds—the marathon runner need waste no effort on rapid acceleration.

Training schedules for cross-country running and long-distance running differ because of the different styles used. A stronger lifting and propulsive action is needed when running over rough terrain than when loping rhythmically along a cinder track or road. Therefore the cross-country runner should build up strength before the season starts and then go for endurance in his running training.

The middle- and long-distance runner performs prolonged repetitive movements against a relatively light resistance. He needs most of all physical and mental stamina plus a reserve of strength to accelerate into a final spurt. Weight training can help considerably to meet all these needs. Stamina can be improved by a routine employing light weights with a high number of repetitions. Leg strength can be gained by exercising with a heavy weight with few repetitions. Mental stamina can also be improved during the training as a direct result of battling with increasing poundages and repetitions. With the knowledge that the training is improving strength and stamina, comes self-confidence in being able to keep going longer. The con-

fidence based on measurable progress in poundage and physical development is a considerable factor influencing mental stamina or the will to keep going and give that little bit extra. Ultimately the best mental stamina will grow out of this self-confidence and out of graded experience in highly competitive and evenly matched races.

The weights used for both strength and stamina training should be very accurately gauged so that the muscles being exercised can only cope with about ten repetitions of the heavy poundages for strength development and with about twenty repetitions for endurance.

Most coaches recommend weight training from November to mid-April. During this period two nights a week can be devoted to weight training whilst on the other training evenings, or on the same evening as the weight training routine, depending on the time available, some roadwork or cross-country running can be done as well. Once the competitive season starts there should be little need for further weight training sessions. By this time strength and stamina should have been adequately developed for serious training on the track.

THE SPRINTS

Which events can now legitimately be called sprints? Twenty years ago the answer would have been simple. The 100 and 200 metres. But now in both the 400 and 800 metres the athlete is in fact almost maintaining his top speed for the whole distance.

Athletes training for the 400 and 800 metres appear to have adopted more rigorous training programmes than have the men concentrating on the 100 metres. Progress has been made by following a training schedule which has given them sufficient endurance to maintain maximum speed over the greater distances. In the 200 metres race there is no evidence to suggest that greater endurance would produce better times. Top-class sprinters slow down so little towards the end of their dash that they cover the 200 metres in a time less than twice that for the 100 metres. True, they have the advantage of entering the second hundred with a flying start, but it does show that they can maintain their fastest speed for a longer distance. If any improvement is to be made then it should not be towards endurance principally that training be directed. The coach must look elsewhere for the weaker aspects of his athletes' sprinting technique.

The start is the obvious place to examine first for signs of inefficient technique. The initial explosive thrust has to be finely timed to coincide with the explosion of the cartridge in the gun. The response must be immediate. Watch a cat poised to pounce on a toy mouse or a bobbin on a string. There are no tensed muscles, it appears to be relaxed, intensely concentrating. The spring comes like a flash of light. The co-ordination of mind and muscle necessary for immediate response can only be acquired by a man who is superbly fit. Physiologists claim that progressive weight training enables the nervous system to discharge motor impulses into the muscles at a greater frequency. A greater proportion of the muscle's fibres can be stimulated too. The muscle, in fact, can react more quickly and with greater force, which is just what a sprinter needs to get him off the starting-blocks in the quickest time. With quicker reactions and more strength he can be off like a bullet and accelerate rapidly.

Training schedules for sprinters should therefore be directed first of all to the development of optimum strength and then towards the co-ordination of mind and muscle for the start and the reciprocal relaxation and good style during the race.

EXERCISES FOR 100 AND 200 METRES

1 *Warm-up:* Jogging and general mobilising exercises followed by a short period of skip jumping to land in crouch position until light perspiration is induced.

2 *Half squats* (knee extensor exercise *1*, page 41): Use a heavy weight which cuts the maximum repetitions to ten. The leg extensors, quadriceps and gluteals are developed with this exercise.

3 *Trunk raising backwards* (dorsal exercise *1*, page 50): Anchor the feet under a strap on the bench. This exercise makes for stability of the shoulder girdle by strengthening the dorsal and posterior deltoid muscles. Use a weight allowing twenty repetitions.

4 *Inclined sit-ups* (abdominal exercise *2*, page 38): The hip flexors are strengthened by this exercise and so help the runner to maintain a high knee lift. The higher the knee is lifted the greater is the momentum and therefore power as the foot comes down and strikes the ground. The weight selected should allow twenty repetitions.

5 *Straight arm pullovers* (chest exercise *1*, page 54): Done correctly this exercise can have a mobilising as well as strengthening effect. The beneficial mobilising effect comes from the 'fanning' out of the rib cage as the weight is lowered overhead. Chest mobility is an aid to respiratory efficiency.

6 *Calf raise* (lower leg exercise *1*, page 48): Keep the knees and back straight and use a very heavy weight so that the maximum repetitions are about eight or ten. Rise as high as possible on the toes and so help to develop fully the muscles which give that final flick to the propulsion initiated by the bigger extensor muscles of the knee and hip.

7 *Step-ups* (general endurance exercise *1*, page 141): This is a first-class exercise for sprinters. It develops the extensors of the leg, the hip flexors responsible for the high knee lift and also general circulatory and respiratory endurance. Use a bench or chair at least 20 inches high.

THE 400 AND 800 METRES

During the early part of the winter conditioning programme, the emphasis in training must still be mainly on strength in order to gain speed, but as the track season approaches a lighter routine using high repetitions and sets should be adopted as a lead into track training for running endurance. The man who seizes a good lead early in the 400 metres race is more likely to keep it if he has superior stamina. Pre-season training must have this twofold aim and progress should be parallel in strength and endurance after the first optimum level has been achieved. Many athletes adopt a heavy and light routine from the beginning of their weight training programme. Some of the exercises are done in sets of heavy weights with low repetitions followed by a set of light weights and a high number of repetitions of the same exercise; other trainers favour the first method of achieving optimum strength before going for endurance. It really is a matter for personal preference, but practically speaking the first method described is the easiest because the barbell poundage need not be altered in between each set of the same exercise.

EXERCISES FOR THE 400 AND 800 METRES

1 *Warm-up:* As for the 100 metres.

2 *Squat jumps* (knee extensors exercise *5*, page 43): Use a light weight allowing sets of twenty repetitions. The shoulders should be well padded to prevent the bar bruising

the vertebrae as it jars down on the landing after each jump. It would be more convenient really to make a padded felt sleeve for the bar than to balance a towel round the neck. This is a strong exercise for the hip, knee and ankle extensors. Medicine balls may also be used as shown on page 123.

3 *Bent arm raise, lying* (chest exercise 6, page 61): A light weight allowing twenty to twenty-five repetitions maximum should be selected. The muscles worked in this exercise are those used in punching the arms across the body.

4 *Inclined sit-ups* (abdominal exercise 2, page 38): Sets of fifteen repetitions maximum should be done.

5 *Calf raise* (lower leg exercise 1, page 48): Remember that some of the effects of this exercise will be lost if the back is not kept erect and the knees straight. Strongly developed calf muscles, particularly gastrocnemius, are responsible for the final 'kick' in the push from the rear leg. It adds distance to the stride—hence speed.

6 *Bench jumps* (leg exercise 2, page 139): Stand astride a low bench or box about 15 inches high, holding dumb-bells by the side or a disc in front of the body. Jump on and off the bench as many times as possible within 30 seconds. During the winter months, this is an ideal way of maintaining a high degree of circulatory and respiratory efficiency. Try to increase the number of jumps performed within the set time of half a minute. When no further increases can be made in the number of repetitions add to the weight carried and build up to a high number of repetitions again.

THE MILE AND LONG-DISTANCE RACES

In the mile the acceleration of the sprinter is needed for finishing bursts and to take tactical advantage of an opponent. Great endurance is needed to retain any advantage that may have been gained. Therefore the training must once more be designed to develop strength and then later be adjusted for endurance. With the longer events the accelerating ability is not as important. For the 5000 and 10000 metres and marathon races, weight training can be used as a foil to training on the track and roads. The following pre-season routine with weights is suggested:

1 *Warm-up:* As for the 100 metres.

2 *Half squats* (knee extensor exercise 1, page 41): Select a heavy poundage allowing only ten repetitions. Avoid leaning forward at the hips. This exercise develops the powerful extensors needed for acceleration.

3 *Leg lifting* (abdominal exercise 6, page 40): Weight an iron boot so that only fifteen to twenty repetitions can be done. Endurance in the hip flexor muscles used in the knee lift are developed in this exercise as well as the abdominals which work statically to stabilise the pelvis and thorax during the exercise.

4 *Burpees* (circuit training exercise *1*, pages 120 and 121): Although this is not a pure weight training exercise, because no iron weights are used, the legs work strongly against the total body weight. Try to do as many complete movements as possible within the prescribed time of half a minute. It is a first-class exercise for developing leg muscles and general endurance.

5 *Straight arm pullovers* (chest exercise *1*, page 54): Done correctly this exercise can have a mobilising as well as a strengthening effect. The beneficial mobilising effect comes from the 'fanning' out of the rib cage as the weight is lowered overhead. Chest mobility helps to improve respiratory efficiency.

6 *Step-ups* (general endurance exercise *1*, page 141): This exercise is worthy of inclusion in any running schedule because of its many meritorious effects. Knee lift is improved by the development of hip flexor stamina, strength is gained in the leg extensors, especially if weights are carried, and, because of the exercising of so many big muscle groups and the demands they make on the heart and lungs, it is an excellent means of developing general endurance. Progress in the exercise should be made by trying to increase the number of complete stepping movements done in the half minute, then extend the time to one minute, and finally add more weight to the exercise by carrying dumb-bells and still aim to reach the same number of total repetitions as before weights were carried.

CROSS-COUNTRY RUNNING

The demands of this type of racing are searching and varied because of the impossibility of maintaining the even expenditure of effort which is possible with every other type of racing whether it be on the road or the track. Runners generally perform better when the pace can be kept regular and the effort planned so that it is spread evenly over the whole distance. With the changes in the terrain and consequent length of stride the degree of effort and pace also change in the cross-country race. To prepare for these distinctive features of the event, training must be adjusted accordingly. Remember that no single exercise can in itself develop more than one particular quality of fitness. Early in the pre-season training the aim should be to strengthen the supporting muscles of the ankle and knee to minimise the risk of strains and injuries in the opening races of the season. After about four weeks of this strengthening routine the emphasis should change. Lighter weights with three or four sets of twenty repetitions should replace the heavy weights and low repetitions. A pre-season conditioning programme could be made up of the following exercises:

1 *Warm-up.*

2 *Half squats* (knee extensors exercise *1*, page 41).

3 *Trunk raising backwards* (dorsal exercise *1*, page 50).

4 *Inclined sit-ups* (abdominal exercise *2*, page 38).

5 *Calf raise* (lower leg exercise *1*, page 48).

6 *Press behind the neck* (arm and shoulder extensor exercise *10*, page 34).

7 *Hack lift* (knee extensor exercise 6, page 43).

It is important to bear in mind that although weight training will develop strength and endurance it is merely a supplement to training in the actual event itself. The athlete should allocate his available training time so that his training programme has a reasonable balance between all the different aspects of physical preparation.

Jumping events

Success in athletic jumping events depends upon a high degree of neuro-muscular co-ordination in order that the competitor can utilise the maximum muscular power available. Unprecedented heights could be attained if the athlete were free to jump as he pleased and were not restricted to passing over a precisely balanced bar set between two uprights.

Because of these curbing factors the high jumper has more to think about than the mere release of an explosive upward thrust. He must gauge his prancing run-up to give him just sufficient forward momentum after the upward jump to carry his body over the plane of the bar, adjust his take-off so that he is in a position to roll or straddle the obstacle and modify his style so that it complies with the

rules. Briefly, then, high jumping requires the accurate co-ordination of three factors:

1 Muscular power.

2 Forward momentum.

3 The mechanics of the take-off.

DISSIPATION OF POWER

There are two main principles to consider in high jumping. Firstly the position of the take-off and secondly the centre of gravity. The more vertical is the take-off the greater is the height attainable from the same power than when the take-off is further from the bar. Secondly, more muscular effort is required to lift the body over the bar in an upright posture than when the body is laid out horizontally because in the latter instance the body's centre of gravity is lower. Muscular power therefore can be dissipated by a poor take-off and an inefficient style. Improvement in muscular power, as with the other events, must go hand-in-hand with improvement in style. In long jumping, greater use may be made of the momentum generated in the run-up. The high jumper normally approaches the bar obliquely with a few prancing steps but the long jumper takes a sufficiently long run-up to build the maximum speed which he can control to hit the board accurately enough with his take-off foot to give him an upward lift and a forward drive. The presence of

Lynn Davies, former Olympic long jump champion, using weights

the take-off board restricts the unfettered release of power and again it is only after long practice that optimum use can be made of the available muscular force.

THE DEVELOPMENT OF POWER FOR JUMPING

The force required to project the body upwards or forwards is directly proportional to the weight of the body. The heavier you are the greater is the power needed. The power is derived primarily from the flexor muscle of the foot, the ankle flexors in the calf, the knee extensors of the quadriceps group and the gluteals of the take-off leg.

But muscles rarely work independently. Prime movers work inefficiently if the fixator and stabilising muscles are not capable of a correspondingly strong contraction. Therefore it would be wrong for jumpers to concentrate entirely on developing the prime mover muscles listed above.

The chest and abdominal muscles also play an important part in the upward thrust, as do the muscles which move the arms and free leg. When the flexors of the hip bring the leg up, the pelvis must be fixed by simultaneous contraction of the abdominals. The upper body, neck and head have to be carefully stabilised in order that the finely balanced posture of the body is not disturbed as it passes over the bar. Long jumpers too must maintain balance during flight to achieve maximum distance and an efficient landing. Pole vaulters require additional strength in the arm, shoulder and abdominal muscles.

It is worth remembering that high-jump and pole-vault

competitions can be long-drawn-out events and an influencing factor in performance is fatigue. For this reason endurance is an aspect of fitness which should not be neglected in training. More than one top-class vaulter has improved his chances in competition through developing endurance in running up and carrying the pole. Some of them have spent long periods running and carrying the pole without vaulting in order to develop stamina in the carrying muscles of the arm and in the legs. The exercises suggested below cater for endurance as well as for power.

SUGGESTED EXERCISES FOR JUMPERS

1 *Leg lifting* (abdominal exercise 6, page 40).
2 *Trunk raising backwards* (dorsal exercise 1, page 50).
3 *Half squats* (knee extensor exercise 1, page 41).
4 *Arms forwards and upwards raise* (elbow flexor exercise 10, page 19).
5 *Trunk curls* (abdominal exercise 1, page 36).
6 *Squat jumps* (circuit training exercise 3, page 123).

SUGGESTED EXERCISES FOR POLE VAULTERS

1 *Calf raise* (lower leg exercise 1, page 48).
2 *Chinning, clasped hands grasp* (elbow flexor exercise 11, page 19).
3 *Head and knee raising* (abdominal exercise 4, page 39).
4 *Trunk and arms raising backwards* (dorsal exercise 2, page 50).
5 *Inclined sit-ups with a twist* (abdominal exercise 3, page 39).
6 *Step-ups* (general endurance exercise 1, page 141).
7 *Deep press-ups* (arm and shoulder extensor exercise 7, page 31).

8 Strength and stamina for sport

THE MAIN physical characteristics of most sports are strength, stamina, speed and agility, coupled with skill in the techniques of the game. But the mere practice or playing of the game does not develop these characteristics to a high degree because during the normal course of play the need for great strength or local muscular endurance arises only at infrequent intervals. The star player is the one with adequate reserves of strength and stamina to meet each one of these occasional demands whilst at the same time maintaining a consistently high level of skill.

Strength required

Some sports require greater strength than others. The canoeist, swimmer and cyclist have to overcome a strong external resistance: the flat blade of the paddle against the water, the cupped hand and resistance of the body through the water, and the force of gravity acting against a cyclist forcing round the pedals up a steep hill. The external forces to be overcome in these sports clearly indicate the need for great strength and muscular endurance.

Other sports require varying degrees of strength. The rugby forward needs power for the pack, the soccer player need not be quite as strong but requires great reserves of stamina to maintain the higher degree of skill required in the game for the full 90 minutes. The boxer needs strong arms and shoulders for punching power and well-developed neck and abdominal muscles to act as shock-absorbers.

To develop the particular strength needed special training is necessary in addition to match practice and play. For example, the basketball shooter or football centre forward who can outjump opponents has a tremendous advantage, but occasions for jumping high do not happen frequently enough during a game for the player to develop the necessary leg power and co-ordination required. Nor would actual practice in jumping develop sufficient leg power, although probably skill in jumping would improve and so add a little more height. But the most marked improvement would be seen after strength in the leg extensor muscles had been developed through special 'resistance-type' exercises.

Similarly, a golf club, tennis racket, cricket and baseball bat can be swung all day without bringing about any noticeable improvement in arm strength. Swimming for hours on end will undoubtedly develop endurance but not the strength to provide the power essential for speed swimming. Strength can only be developed beyond a certain point by exercising muscles against a heavy resistance or an immovable object. Weight training utilises the resistance of iron discs, whilst isometric exercise employs the fixed resistance of opposing muscle groups, walls, or any immovable object.

The value of leg strength

For most sports leg strength is beneficial. When a tennis player turns suddenly and dashes to the opposite side of the court he is changing the direction of a projectile weighing perhaps 180 lb—his body. To make such movements precisely at speed is an asset which enables a good player to retrieve shots which a weaker one would leave as unplayable. (See also 'Sprinting', pages 92 to 93.)

Strength for stability

Not quite so obvious is the need for strength in the muscles controlling posture. They too must be strong for good performance in sport. Particularly important are the back, neck and abdominal muscles for they stabilise the body in a variety of action postures whilst the principal efforts of hitting, throwing or jumping are made by other muscle groups.

Unwanted movements in golf strokes occur with the beginner because of involuntary reactions of the neuro-muscular system brought about by the stimulation of the muscles making the stroke. Yet the golfer has an advantage over other sportsmen in that he makes his own conditions for the stroke. He has as much time as he wants to adjust his stance, consider the swing and all the factors which determine the direction, flight and speed he imparts to the ball. Despite the opportunity for making these preparations, unwanted body movements still occur with the weaker player and impair his shot. How much more likely then are such distracting movements in games which involve rapid reaction to a ball or shuttlecock moving in a wide variety of directions and at different speeds? A high degree of skill is needed to co-ordinate all muscles and strength is required to fix the body in flight or in the stretched positions from which shots are made. You may only be hitting a feather-weight shuttlecock but your back and neck muscles are supporting a head and trunk which weigh heavily.

The head position determines the way your body moves in flight. If a cat is dropped upside down the first movement made by the cat would be of its head to bring about the other body changes needed for regaining a landing position on its feet. Divers, gymnasts, and free-fall parachutists learn how movement of the head and limbs alter body position in flight. To make a winning stroke your body must be in the best possible position for the application of force before the striking action is begun. This is accomplished by good footwork and by having the body firmly stabilised by well-developed muscles. Strong postural muscles respond well to reflex stimuli and make possible shots which weaker players fail to achieve mainly because the body is in a disadvantageous position when the stroke is attempted.

When considering body movement in different positions and the muscle action involved, the pull of gravity must always be borne in mind. For instance, little effort is needed to pull the head and spine backwards when standing but very much more muscular strength is needed to carry out the same movement when the trunk is stretched horizontally forward.

The more that muscle action in sport is analysed the more obvious is the need for general muscular strength. Even in sports which may appear to be less vigorous, increased strength will usually improve performance. For example, in rifle shooting, muscular strength leads to better scores because the arms can be held steady whilst the aim is taken. Professional ballroom dancers also find strength and stamina an asset. Competitions are very long and tiring. Those who can defer the distractions of fatigue are able to maintain perfect co-ordination and grace of movement for the extra critical minutes which may make all the difference between winning and being a runner-up.

The weight training and isometric exercises described on pages 15 to 61 and 143 to 194 can be used to develop the general strength and particular power required for different sports.

Pre-season training

Ankles and knee joints are susceptible to early season injuries and although, thanks to overseas tours, the off-season for soccer players is often very short, it is still worth players' while to spend time in strengthening the muscles supporting the joints which are subjected to the great strain of sudden turns when the foot is partly fixed in the ground by studs.

The quadriceps muscles in particular soon show signs of atrophy when exercise stops and players should not expect their joints to be as strong at the beginning of the season, after a summer spent in rest and inactivity, as they were at the end of the previous one. A few minutes spent daily on exercises with weighted boots or in barbell squats can save weeks lost through early season injuries.

A word of warning

Some sportsmen and athletes try to develop strength for a particular sport by practising with a heavier golf club, racket, discus or bat, believing that the increased weight will develop strength exactly where it is most required. For example, baseball players and cricketers have tried to strengthen the wrist and forearm muscles by practising strokes with a bat made heavier by the insertion of lead. Sometimes success is claimed for the method but at other times performance appears to deteriorate.

Physiologists explain this deterioration by the fact that the complex pattern of the movement has been disturbed. Sports skills are usually controlled automatically by the brain. Information about the pace of the ball, direction of the wind, the position of opponents and the player himself, is received by the central nervous system and fed to the brain which initiates reflex action. Every factor affects the direction and power of the stroke to be made. If the weight of the racket is altered then the whole pattern of movement must be adjusted. For example, less power need be imparted to a stroke played by a heavy racket than a light one because of the increased momentum gained with the extra weight. There is no time for conscious thought when making strokes and if the reflex pattern of movement is disturbed then control is not as accurate and skill consequently deteriorates.

If a player practises with a much heavier implement than usual then muscle groups not normally used may become involved. For example, to swing a heavily weighted cricket or baseball bat the larger muscles of the back begin to take some load off the smaller forearm muscles. The stance and technique of the stroke is thereby altered and automatic control affected.

Conventional weight training and isometric exercises do not interfere with the pattern of complex skills and can develop all the strength a player needs.

There is no room for doubt: the stronger you are, the better you play from the beginning to the end of the season.

9 Weight training for improving sports performance

NOT MANY years ago it was popularly believed that heavily muscled men were 'slow and clumsy', 'muscle bound' or 'tightened up'. Consequently footballers, tennis, rugby, and hockey players were hesitant about using weights to prepare themselves physically for sport. But, during the last ten years, physical fitness tests carried out in Russia, the United States, Germany and Great Britain have refuted the 'muscle-bound' theory and shown it to be a belief based on ignorance and ill-informed opinion.

Further experiments have revealed that some of the massively muscled wrestlers, shot putters and weight lifters score better on the speed tests of muscle reaction than sprinters and jumpers of the more wiry body type formerly accepted as being quick and nimble. Bulky muscles do not necessarily mean slow reactions and coaches now agree that there is a close correlation between increased strength and improved performance in sport. No longer is the weight lifter an oddity.

Some games, such as rugby, present players with more opportunities than others for improving power and strength. In the scrum, for example, leg and back muscles work against maximum resistance provided by efforts of opposing players. But such strengthening activity occurs only during the playing season. To ensure optimum physical development, pre-season training is essential. Otherwise the season would be partly over before players reached peak fitness.

Teams that win championships must be at match fitness the day the competitive programme begins. How is this to be achieved without involving excessive training time during the rest months? Physiologists declare that weight training is probably the most effective method when all factors, especially differences in motivation, are considered.

Basic strengthening routines

The aim during the first phase of training for all games should be to increase general muscle strength through a well-balanced weight training schedule. Beginners should adjust the poundage to suit their own abilities remembering that physical development depends on gradually increasing the resistance on the bar rather than on increasing the number of repetitions. Once more than twelve repetitions can be comfortably done then the poundage must be increased.

The exercises in the basic strengthening schedule below are numbered in the order in which they should be per-

formed. Do three sets of the fixed number of exercises before passing on to the next muscle group to be worked. The schedule should be done once every other day except on the seventh day of training which should be set aside for testing maximum performance, when you should add weights to the bar and count the number of repetitions that you can do before the movements become jerky. Let this new maximum at the increased poundage be the set task for the exercise in the coming week.

SUGGESTED ROUTINE FOR BEGINNERS

The exercises are described fully with illustrations in chapter 4. The exact reference is given in brackets after each exercise below.

1 *Alternate arm curls* (elbow flexor exercise 6, page 18).

2 *Trunk curls* (abdominal exercise *1*, page 36).

3 *Two-hand press* (arm and shoulder extensor exercise *11*, page 35).

4 *Half squats* (knee extensor exercise *1*, page 41).

5 *Trunk raising backwards* (dorsal exercise *1*, page 50): This exercise is more effective if the trunk is lowered down so that only the nose can lightly touch the floor. The back muscles are then kept tensed for the whole set of repetitions

and before relaxing as the body weight is allowed to rest on the floor.

6 *Bench press* (chest exercise *4*, page 58): This is an ideal way of building wide square pectorals and prominent frontal fibres of the deltoids. It is also one of the few exercises for developing the 'pushing muscle'—the serratus anterior—those finger-like bulges which stand out from the side of the chest like extra ribs.

7 *Step-ups* (general endurance exercise *1*, page 141): This is a superb exercise for general physical development. Not only does it provide exercise for all the leg muscles—which after all account for more than two-thirds of the total muscle mass of the body—but it also exercises the heart and lungs. The massive muscular work of the legs stimulates the respiratory and circulatory systems into greatly increased activity and ultimately the heart muscle becomes bigger and stronger, as also do the respiratory muscles of the chest. Do the exercise for half a minute with the left leg leading and then for half a minute with the right leading. If you find the exercise exhausting, try it without weights until you are stronger and fitter.

A MORE ADVANCED STRENGTHENING SCHEDULE

Use either the 'sequence' or the 'three sets' system for this schedule. The final exercise is a taxing one for the respiratory system and it is best left until the end so as not to interfere with the more specific exercises.

1 *Arm curls* (elbow flexor exercise *1*, page 15).

2 *Inclined curls* (abdominal exercise *2*, page 38): Look at the illustration and note that the range of movement is very small but the abdominals are under tension the whole time. If you were to sit up too far forward or to lie down on the ground they would relax in between each repetition and this should be avoided. Place your hand on your mid section and feel how the muscles go slack as you sit in the upright or lying position.

3 *Standing single arm triceps extension* (arm and shoulder extensor exercise *1*, page 26).

4 *Hack lift* (knee extensor exercise *6*, page 43).

5 *Trunk and arms raising backwards* (dorsal exercise *2*, page 50): This exercise involves a strong contraction of the dorsal extensor muscles as well as those of the arm and shoulder group.

6 *Bent arm raise, lying* (chest exercise *6*, page 61).

7 *Squat jumps* (knee extensor exercise *5*, page 43).

Soccer training with weights

The soccer player needs strength for power and the stamina to maintain a very high degree of skill for the full 90 minutes plus the extra time he may have to play in some crucial matches. When stamina is lacking, fatigue soon begins to impair performance.

Power, the combination of strength and speed, is essential for sudden acceleration and changes of direction, for jumping high to head a ball when harassed by opposing players and, of course, for shooting hard.

The need for this strength and stamina explains why weights are now used so much in the soccer player's fitness training programme.

Heavy weights which allow a maximum of ten repetitions are used for developing strength whilst lighter weights with a high number of repetitions are needed for stamina development.

When preparing the fitness training programme we must remember that there are two kinds of stamina to be developed. There is the stamina which calls for general endurance of the heart, lungs and circulatory systems and there is also the stamina dependent on local muscular endurance.

Intense physical exertion which causes the heart and lungs to work maximally over a long period brings on the general fatigue we can see in the player forcing himself to run whilst nearing a stage of complete collapse.

Local muscular endurance is needed when a group of muscles must maintain a prolonged sequence of rapid contractions. This, for example, is what happens to the calf muscles in running. They have to contract and relax in rapid succession with little time for recovery and the elimination of the waste products of fatigue. Eventually these muscles fail to respond to the nervous stimulus and further work is impossible. Sometimes the accumulation of waste products causes the muscles to go into a painful spasm of contraction, cramp. Thus we can have local muscular exhaustion when the player is otherwise fit to carry on playing vigorously.

To achieve the general and local endurance, the strength, speed and power needed by the top-class footballer, the following forms of training are recommended:
Circuit training (see circuit on pages 119 to 129).
Obstacle course (see course on page 107).
Weight training for general strength (see routine below).

WEIGHT TRAINING ROUTINE FOR SOCCER PLAYERS
1 *Hack lift* (knee extensor exercise 6, page 43).
2 *Trunk curls* (abdominal exercise 1, page 36).
3 *Calf raise* (lower leg exercise 1, page 48).
4 *Trunk raising backwards* (dorsal exercise 1, page 50).
5 *The snatch from the 'hang' position* (general endurance exercise 7, page 142).
6 *Squat jumps* (knee extensor exercise 5, page 43).

AN OBSTACLE COURSE FOR SOCCER PLAYERS
The obstacle course is a purposeful form of training which brings interest and variety into the programme. The

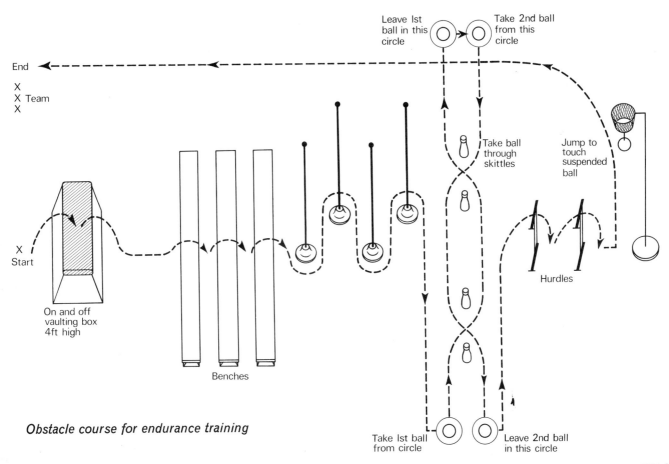

Leave lst ball in this circle

Take 2nd ball from this circle

End

X
X Team
X

Take ball through skittles

Jump to touch suspended ball

X Start

On and off vaulting box 4ft high

Benches

Hurdles

Take lst ball from circle

Leave 2nd ball in this circle

Obstacle course for endurance training

movement and agility involved develop the strength, co-ordination and local endurance needed in the game itself. Players under training can be grouped into teams of four or six and the course completed in relay fashion so that one team competes against another. The course should be made severe enough to elicit maximum effort for between 30 and 40 seconds. Thus, with a team of four, the individual works maximally for 30 seconds and then has 90 seconds rest waiting for the other three to complete the course before starting his second lap. For players who are in a good state of training eight or ten laps should be the initial aim. Teams can be reduced to shorten the rest period, or the course made more severe if players are able to complete it in less than 30 seconds. (See course on page 107.)

Rugby

Quick bursts of power terminating in a tackle require strength for acceleration and for driving into physical contact with the opposing player. The muscle groups needing special attention are the extensors of the back, neck, hip, knee and ankle. These are the muscles which provide the forward thrust against stiff resistance.

For strength in tackling, strong flexors of the arm and hand are needed, so that once a player is firmly grasped he can be held and brought down.

Although the style of running in rugby differs in some respects from that of soccer the power is furnished from the same muscle groups—the extensors of the hip, knee and ankle. There is a tendency for rugby players to run with shorter steps and with knees rarely fully extended. To improve power in side stepping the abductors and adductors of the leg need some special attention. A point also to remember is that these are the muscles most likely to suffer from strains and tears during the early part of the season. The stretch and strengthen principle should be applied to these muscles (see chapter 13, page 144).

Pre-season training should include a basic strengthening routine such as the one described on page 104, cross-country running, zig-zag running in short bursts on the field, dropping, rolling, recovering quickly and running again. A useful exercise for developing stamina is skipping with a rope and this can be included in a stamina training circuit. (See exercises for general endurance in chapter 12.)

WEIGHT TRAINING FOR RUGBY

1 *Arm curls* (elbow flexor exercise *1*, page 15).

2 *Squat jumps* (knee extensor exercise *5*, page 43).

3 *Inclined sit-ups or curls with a twist* (abdominal exercise *3*, page 39).

4 *Leg abduction* (knee extensor exercise *4*, page 43).

5 *Bench press* (chest exercise *4*, page 58).

6 *Trunk and arms raising backwards* (dorsal exercise *2*, page 50).

7 *Lunging* (knee extensor exercise *9*, page 47).

Swimming

Competitive swimming calls for strong muscles, a high degree of general endurance and supple joints. Because of this need for flexibility some swimming coaches were reluctant to recommend weight training as part of the physical preparation for the season's programme, but in recent years more and more countries have adopted weight training and it is perhaps significant that as the conditioning schedules became more intensive, swimming records of long standing were broken by almost unbelievable margins.

No matter how many hours a swimmer may spend in the water his strength will not increase much after a certain level has been reached. This is because the resistance provided by the water remains the same.

Drogues and sea anchors have been tried in order to increase this water resistance but such methods have not been given the accolade of acceptance. There is also always the risk of a swimmer altering an effective style in order to cope with the unnatural resistance in the water, just as a golfer spoils his swing by training with a much heavier club than he would normally use. Weight training is the only sure way of developing the strength and endurance required for optimum performance.

The swimmer contemplating top-class competition must aim for great strength in all the muscle groups. Speed is not possible without strength. The two combined give the power needed for explosive bursts of acceleration.

TRAINING PROGRAMME FOR SWIMMING

Before each weight training session a thorough warming-up and mobilising routine should be completed. It is perhaps more important for swimmers to recognise the importance of suppling exercises before weight training than it is for any other sport. (See also the stretch and strengthen principle in chapter 13, page 144.)

MOBILISING EXERCISES USING LIGHT WEIGHTS

1 *Double arm circling* holding 10-lb disc in each hand (exercise 2, page 5).
2 *Trunk and arm circling* holding 10-lb disc with both hands (exercise 4, page 5).
3 *Trunk bending sideways* (dorsal exercise 7, page 53).
4 *Lever rotation* (forearm exercise 6, page 25).
5 *Standing triceps extension with barbell* (arm and shoulder extensor exercise 2, page 26).
6 *Lunging* (knee extensor exercise 9, page 47).

EXERCISES FOR STRENGTH DEVELOPMENT

1 *Arm curls* (elbow flexor exercise 1, page 15).
2 *Squat jumps* (knee extensor exercise 5, page 43).
3 *Inclined curls or sit-ups* (abdominal exercise 2, page 38).
4 *Trunk and arms raising backwards* (dorsal exercise 2, page 50).
5 *Double bent arm pullovers* (chest exercise 3, page 56).
6 *Upright rowing* (shoulder flexors and abductors exercise 2, page 21).

7 *Leg lifting* and *leg extensions* (knee extensor exercises *2* and *3*, page 42).

8 *Bench press* (chest exercise *4*, page 58).

Ideally weight training should begin about three months before the competition season opens and gradually the time spent in the gymnasium should be reduced and more time devoted to water practices and mobilising exercises. Road-work, jogging, should be done during the pre-season training along with weight training, and use should also be made of the basic isometric exercises which develop and maintain strength without inducing fatigue (see chapters 13 to 16 inclusive).

Canoeing

For canoeing, where even greater strength is needed in order to draw the broad blade cleanly through the water without wavering, the training schedule should include a very heavy routine in the non-racing months which tapers off to lighter weights and perhaps circuit-type training for endurance as the competitive season approaches and more time is spent in the water.

Ray Blick, former British Olympic 10000 metres finalist, recommends this routine: start at the end of September when competitive racing has finished and quickly work up to a routine using very heavy weights with five or less repetitions. Keep to this heavy routine until about Christmas,

Ray Blick, who represented Great Britain in the Olympic canoe events at Melbourne and Rome, recommends weight and circuit training to build up muscular power, strength and stamina before the competition canoe racing season begins.

training four days a week. In about January, or February at the latest, according to the water conditions, begin to paddle over long distances. The weight training supplements the water training. Still work for development of strength until around March and then begin to introduce circuit training with a bias towards endurance rather than pure strength. Use lighter weights and more repetitions, in the region of twenty as compared with the fives and sevens for the heavier weights. Do three laps of an eight-exercise circuit performing three-quarters of maximum repetitions on each exercise every lap. During the height of the competitive season in June, July and August, paddling should take preference over all other types of training. Spend at least three hours a day on the water and do a circuit twice a week.

Ray Blick's recommended weight training routine includes the following exercises:

1 *Bench press* (chest exercise *4*, page *58*).

2 *Parallel bar dips* (arm and shoulder extensor exercise *5*, page *30*).

3 *Straight arm pullovers* (chest exercise *1*, page *54*).

4 *Inclined curls* (abdominal exercise *2*, page *38*).

5 *Trunk raising backwards* (dorsal exercise *1*, page *50*).

6 *Double leg lift and cross over* (abdominal exercise *8*, page *40*).

7 *Rope climbing without using feet:* This is listed as a chest exercise (*2* and *3*, page *133*), but Blick recommends climbing in order to strengthen the grip. The gripping muscles of the forearm are the weakest link in the chain of muscles which pull the paddle.

Basketball

To perform the basic ball skills of basketball may appear to require little strength but to execute them accurately during the fierce competition of a game demands both muscular power and stamina.

For a player who has the height but not the strength, weight training is an essential part of the complete physical conditioning programme. Playing the game itself does not develop the power needed for jumping, pivoting and moving the body with sure control. It is a fact that many basketball players have increased their score on the vertical jump test by as much as 6 inches after a period of general weight training. Suggested schedules are described on pages 104 to 105.

A training circuit which includes a shuttle run and the bench-jump exercise should develop the endurance needed to maintain accuracy in the skills for the full period of the game (see chapter 12).

Tennis, badminton and squash

For many years world champion racket players have trained with weights in order to develop the strength needed for controlling body posture in movement and for adding power to their strokes. (Jonah Barrington of Great Britain, the world squash champion, uses both weight training and circuit training.)

When all unwanted body movements are eliminated due to the increased stability of joints controlled by the postural muscles, strokes may be executed more accurately.

The development of wrist strength, grip, a powerful forehand drive in tennis and the serve is discussed in greater detail in chapter 14—Isometric exercise for improving sports performance. The isometric exercises recommended in this chapter are an ideal complement to the general weight training routines described on pages 104 to 105.

10 Training for stamina

SPORTSMEN AND women who reach the heights of physical achievement have invariably more than skill and muscular ability. They have a marked degree of mental toughness too. It is a quality ingrained in every champion, partly bred in the bone and partly developed through a long conditioning process. There is no easy way to the top: it is a hard grind in which muscles have to be worked to their limits in a rigorous training programme and the mind taught to push the body on despite discomfort and feelings of fatigue.

When the mind becomes accustomed to rejecting the alarm signals flashing from tired muscles wanting to rest, distress symptons fade and the body, which always seems to underrate its own ability, forges ahead to greater feats still. The mountaineer can force his way through driving snow and blasting wind to conquer the peaks, the long-distance runner fight to the finishing tape, the fast bowler put every ounce of effort into each delivery and the tennis champion play his opponent into the ground. They know they can carry on for they have done it before, learned to ignore the distractions of physical distress, pain and fatigue. It is this quality, this complex blend of physical and mental endurance, that distinguishes the star from the average performer.

The knowledge gained from the experience of rigorous endurance training develops self-confidence which then in turn encourages the athlete to make additional demands upon his body even though his lungs feel fit to burst and his heart is pounding in his ears. Half the battle is won when the mind believes that its body is capable of doing what it is asked to do and more.

The chief aim of stamina training is to improve circulatory and respiratory efficiency. Rigorous exercise for the large muscle groups of the body is the way this is usually achieved for, as muscles burn up energy, increasing demands are made for the fuel and oxygen carried to active muscles by the blood. The lungs work harder to re-oxygenate it and the heart pumps more rapidly and strongly to drive the oxygen-laden blood to tiring tissues.

The leg muscles, which comprise two-thirds of the body's total muscle mass, are those usually exercised most thoroughly in endurance training. Long-distance running, without doubt, is one of the best ways of developing general organic efficiency and endurance but when, for practical reasons, running is not possible, there are alternative exercises such as those used in the circuit training schedules described on pages 141 to 142.

Middle- and long-distance runners who have broken world records in recent years employ a combination of weight training, circuit training and running. Sometimes the running may take the form of fast laps of a track with intervals of slow laps between the fast ones, running up steep soft sandhills, or jogging over fells. Mountaineering has also been used by well-known international athletes in training for events needing endurance. These, and similar activities, create demands upon the circulatory and respiratory systems which consequently develop to cope with the tasks asked of them.

Endurance training can be boring, long periods of training are necessary to build stamina and consequently variety must be introduced into the training schedule. The conditioning programme needs to be varied enough to keep the mind alert and each individual interested in his own reactions.

Gradually, as a result of regular endurance training, changes take place in the body. The heart muscle responds to overload in the same way as the skeletal muscles, by becoming bigger and stronger. Hypertrophy, as this growth is called, is a natural and beneficial development which enables the heart to pump a greater volume of blood into the arteries with each beat: its stroke volume is raised. Consequently, the resting heart rate drops. That of a long-distance runner in training may be in the lower forties whilst that of the untrained man is usually between sixty and seventy beats per minute. The same sort of reaction has been found in tests done on animals—the more active ones have larger hearts than those that don't run about so much.

Greyhounds, for example, have larger hearts than pet house-dogs of the same size.

The enlarged heart, satisfying normal requirements with a slow resting beat, has a greater reserve (cardiac reserve) to call upon when the demands of strenuous exertion need to be met by an increase in blood flow. Furthermore, whilst the heart rate of the untrained man must increase rapidly to cope with any additional physical activity, the heart of the trained man uses its capacity for maximal dilation and the rate does not need to increase as much in meeting the same output requirements.

Another way in which the circulatory system improves through training is by developing the capability of opening up more capillaries within working muscles. This allows energy fuel and oxygen to be more readily available and it also facilitates the elimination of waste products of fatigue.

Prolonged periods of stamina training bring corresponding improvements in the respiratory system. Vital capacity, the difference in volume between maximum expiration and maximum inspiration, improves after a regular exercise programme. By extreme comparison the vital capacity of people who are incapacitated by injury and are bed-ridden, decreases. Although there is conflicting evidence on the value of the vital capacity figure as a general index of fitness there is no doubt that in certain activities, such as long-distance running and swimming, a large vital capacity is highly desirable.

With increased vital capacity comes a reduction in the resting rate of breathing due to the larger absorptive surface of the lungs and also to the improvement in pulmonary circulation, both of which contribute to a more speedy and efficient exchange of carbon dioxide and oxygen.

The highly trained athlete may have a resting respiratory rate as low as eight times a minute as compared with eighteen times a minute of an untrained man.

For the performance of the same given amount of work, experiments have shown that the athlete who has undergone rigorous stamina-type training takes in a smaller volume of air than the untrained man. This seems to indicate that stamina training develops a more efficient system for the oxygenation of blood. More oxygen is absorbed from a given volume of air breathed.

Apart from the changes in the lungs, there is another reason for the improvement in respiratory efficiency: the development of the diaphragm and the ancillary muscles of respiration.

One of the incidental improvements resulting from endurance training, which is often overlooked, is that in carrying out prolonged exercise any excessive stores of body fat are consumed. Fat carried in and around muscle fibres impairs efficiency and limits performance in activities demanding stamina, except perhaps in swimming where its presence is often an integral part of the body type from which good swimmers are drawn. Long-distance swimmers in particular need an adequate covering of subcutaneous fat to insulate the body from cold water and cut down heat loss.

But, generally, for the sportsman excess fat is a handicap.

We know that the mind can be educated to withstand the discomfort of fatigue and that muscles can be trained to a pitch of efficiency capable of performing remarkable feats, but the ultimate achievement in endurance activities depends upon the will to succeed, to win or to survive when the situation is desperate. The motivating force is of paramount importance. Ambition, anger, fear and pride can push the body to its limits and no matter how hard an athlete may have trained, if he is apathetic towards victory he is not going to make the best use of the physical qualities that his training has developed. The sportsman or athlete who wants to be a champion must find a driving purpose, an inspired reason, for winning.

11 Circuit training

CIRCUIT TRAINING is probably the most significant contribution that has been made to physical education in Great Britain for many years. It is popular, purposeful and effective. From its inception at Leeds University where it developed as a voluntary fitness training activity, it has spread to secondary schools, football and athletic clubs, keep-fit classes for businessmen, medical rehabilitation centres and to all three of the armed services. It is not only widely adopted in Great Britain but also in many parts of the world.

What is circuit training?

As the name implies it is a form of training that involves going round a sequence of exercises (usually between six and twelve) one after the other with a short pause between each. Individuals do a set number of repetitions at each exercise until they come to the first exercise again and start a second lap.

The exercises are specially selected so that a fixed amount

of effort is required on each one. This might be measured by the number of repetitions, the resistance or load provided for the muscles to work against, or a time factor for the completion of the whole schedule. Exercises must be simple and involve very little skill. Two or three circuits, or laps of the exercises, constitute a training session, and as training progresses the improvement in strength and stamina may be seen in the increase of repetitions, the heavier poundage used or the decrease in the overall time taken for three laps of the circuit.

Circuit training is an aspect of physical education which is almost a subject in itself and teachers are advised to read the standard book on the subject, *Circuit Training*, written by the originators of the idea, R. E. Morgan and G. T. Adamson.[1]

Preparing a circuit

Circuit training is used mainly to develop general endurance and basic strength but if a high degree of strength is required then heavier weights must be used with fewer repetitions according to normal weight training practice. With circuit training, exercises can be selected to give a special bias to particular aspects of fitness depending upon the aim of the training and the physical condition of the trainee. Coaches can devise circuits to develop strength, power, endurance and even skill under stress.

For all-round physical development, exercises are usually selected to work all of the major muscle groups, such as the arm flexors, arm extensors, leg, dorsal, abdominal and chest groups. The circuit should also include exercises for general respiratory and circulatory endurance. The best exercises for this type of development are those involving massive movements and calling for great effort from the leg muscles (which comprise two-thirds of the total muscle mass of the body) and as many of the other muscles of the body as possible. Typical exercises for the development of cardio-vascular-respiratory endurance are the *Burpees* and *Step-ups* exercises (pages 120 to 121, 141).

No single exercise can develop both strength and endurance equally well at the same time, and it is for this reason that general fitness training circuits should include some exercises which call for many repetitions with comparatively light resistance to develop endurance and some with a weight resistance that allows only a few repetitions in order to increase muscular strength.

Training rate

When circuit training was first introduced the task at each exercise was fixed for each individual by his performance of maximum repetitions at a separate testing session in which there was a short rest and recovery period in between every exercise. One half or two-thirds of a trainee's maximum repetitions for each exercise was the task usually set for training. He was then given a card like the one shown below, completed according to his test performance.

CIRCUIT TRAINING CARD

NAME. . . . .

Exercise	max. reps.	trg. task	max. reps.	trg. task	max. reps.	trg. task	max. reps.	trg. task
1. Fall hanging, chinning								
2. Towel placing on chair								
3. Trunk raising backwards with medicine ball								
4. Shuttle run								
5. Double leg lift								
6. Half squat								
7. Rope climb								
8. Vest or towel straddle								
Date of tests								

All these exercises are described in greater detail on pages 130 to 143.

But during the last few years circuit training has changed considerably. More exercises have been added to the basic ones recommended by Morgan and Adamson and further fields of profitable application have been found.

The individualised form of training described above found few advocates on the Continent. Simpler systems were necessary in order to allow groups of varying ability to train regularly and at the same time with minimal administrative interference. Experience showed that it was rarely necessary to measure each individual's performance and set his training task accordingly. Instead, broad bands of training tasks were fixed to suit the approximate ability of participants.

When they can complete the circuit without undue exhaustion, progress can be made by:

1 Increasing the repetitions in each exercise, *or*
2 Increasing the resistance provided by the exercise, *or*
3 Reducing the time taken for the complete circuit.

When the first method of progression is used the increased task should be done, if possible, in the same time as the original circuit. Exercises may be made more severe by adding weight or altering the starting position so that more body weight provides the resistance to the working muscles—as, for example, when the feet are raised in the press-ups exercise, more weight is thrown upon the arm extensor muscles. The simplest method of making progress with a group of trainees who are at a similar stage of fitness training, such as may be found in a club soccer or basketball team, is by reducing the time taken to do the complete circuit. The equipment for each exercise remains the same and each individual tries to reduce his own time for the schedule. Sometimes the equipment can be duplicated so that a harder circuit can be done by the stronger boys and the less severe one by those who are not quite so fit. Some clubs and schools have 'green', 'blue' and 'red' circuits with trainees progressing through the easier grades to the hardest.

Organisation of circuit training

Until individuals are well acquainted with circuit training schedules it is worthwhile having a large numbered picture for every point on the circuit. Pin drawings or enlarged photographs, with two or three clear instructions printed below, can save a lot of explanations to trainees who are not clear where to go next and what to do. Photographs are better than drawings for showing clearly the correct positions for each part of the exercise.

Once the intensity of exercise has been fixed for each group then the coach or teacher gives the signal to start. A whistle blast is effective for starting and stopping work. Initially it is safer to use a 20-second stint of work followed by 20 seconds for rest and movement to the next exercise station on the circuit. With fitter athletes the exercise period can be extended to 30 seconds. The duration of exercise depends also upon sex (women and girls should work well within their physical capacities), age (special care should be taken with those over forty), physical condition (exercise for people with infections can be hazardous) and length of circuit (in a circuit of fifteen exercises a 20-second exercise period is advisable).

When circuit training is taken in schools it is usually advisable to leave the circuit for the end of the period so that boys finish on it as a climax to the lesson. They will usually be sweating profusely and ready to retire to the showers. They will certainly not be in a receptive mood for learning new skills. Fatigue distracts the class from the coach and half-hearted efforts would be made.

On the other hand there is something to be said for practising skills after a circuit training session, especially in those sports which demand the maintenance of a high degree of skill even when players are very tired. A team trained in this way can face 'extra time' more confidently after a gruelling 90 minutes of cup-tie football.

There is always a temptation for boys and men working as individuals to make straight for the apparatus when it is set out as a circuit. Coaches and teachers must insist on a thorough warm-up session before starting strenuous exercise.

Fourteen or fifteen is the best age to introduce circuit training in schools. Boys are beginning to pay more attention to their physical development and comparative strength. Progress, which is readily seen, is a good incentive and in boarding schools voluntary evening training has proved itself to be a popular activity. Care however should be taken to ensure that boys do not overstrain. Many will want to keep up with colleagues in the class and there is danger here for the weaker boy.

The attraction of circuit training

Circuit training provides a positive stimulus to further effort because progress can be measured so easily. Boys in particular like to have targets to aim at and gain enormous satisfaction from achievement. The strong and the not quite so strong can derive just the same gratification in watching the improvement in their performance.

With voluntary circuit training individuals can work according to their own schedule and yet feel they are part of one group working together.

A suggested circuit for 13 to 18 year olds

The following exercises are explained and illustrated on pages 120 to 129:

1 *Burpees.*
2 *High front support.*
3 *Squat jumps.*
4 *Medicine ball throw.*
5 *Inclined curls.*
6 *Standing jump over rope and crawl back under.*
7 *Heaving on the beam.*
8 *Low box or bench skipping.*

REFERENCE
1 R. E. Morgan, B.A. and G. T. Adamson, B.Sc., *Circuit Training* (Bell).

1 *Burpees:* **This is a four-count exercise. Stand, drop into crouch position on 'one' with hands flat on the floor.**

Thrust both legs backwards into the front support position on the count 'two'.

Jump the legs forward on the count 'three', and stand up on 'four'.

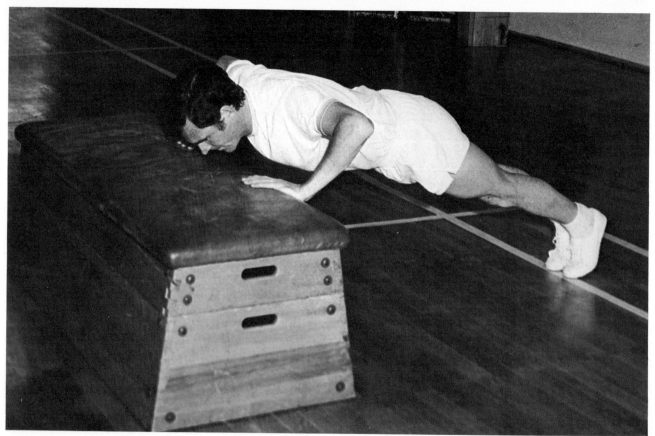

2 *High front support:* Arm bending and stretching.

3 *Squat jumps:* Adopt a full knees-bend position and hold a medicine ball under each arm. Jump upwards clear of the ground and straighten the legs. Land lightly to drop into the knees-bend position and repeat. Demonstrated here by Graham Beckwith, formerly Great Britain's Olympic basketball centre.

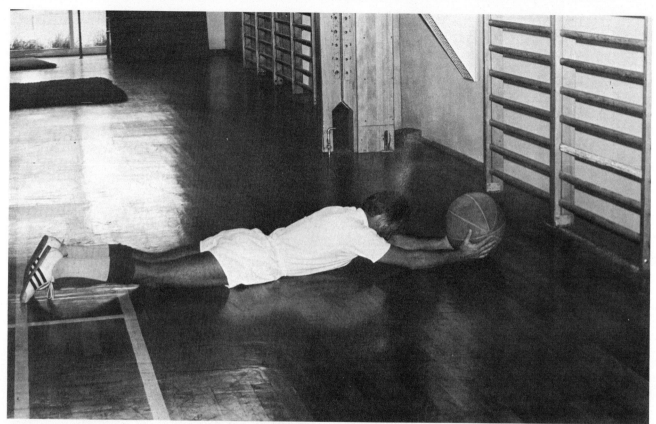

4 *Medicine ball throw:* From prone lying the individual throws the ball over the wall-bar marked with chalk. This should be about 20 inches from the ground. Recover ball and repeat.

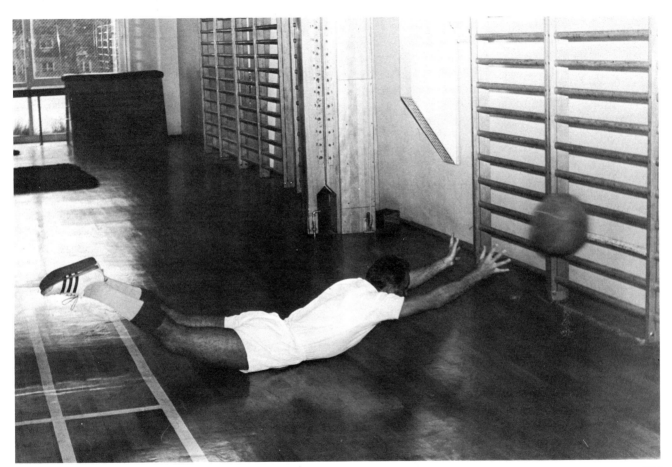

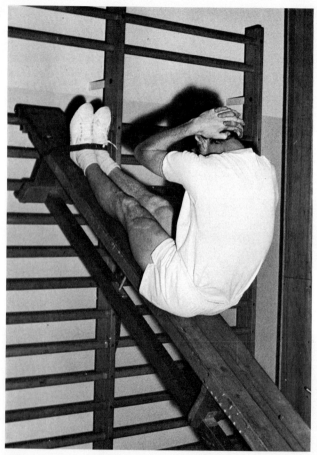

5 *Inclined curls:* Hands behind head, feet under strap passing around bench as shown on the left. Curl upwards to press the head close to the knees (see also page 38).

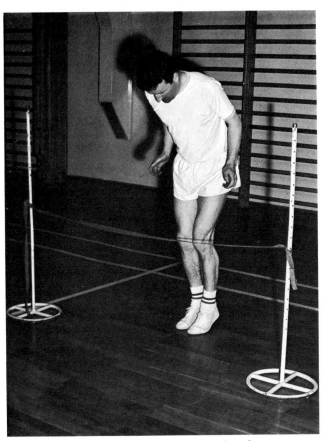

6 *Standing jump over rope and crawl back under.*

7 *Heaving on the beam:* Grasp the beam, which should be at comfortable stretch height, as shown in the photograph on the left. Bend arms to raise chin to beam.

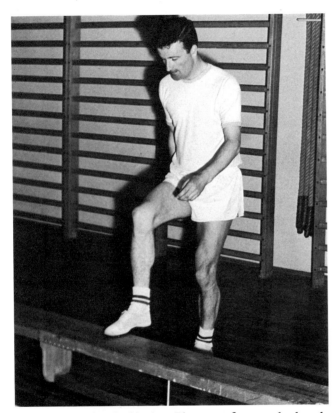

8 *Low box or bench skipping:* Place one foot on the bench and one on the floor. In one movement change feet. Complete as many changes as possible.

12 Circuit training exercises

NEARLY ALL load-resisting exercises are suitable for inclusion in a circuit but some are more suitable than others. The basic principles to guide selection are that the exercises should:

1 Require little skill and be known to the class.
2 Be easily measured in terms of time or repetitions.
3 Induce fatigue within half a minute.
4 Affect large muscle groups.
5 Be easily duplicated so that bottlenecks do not arise from waiting for a turn on the equipment.
6 Give the particular bias to the circuit according to the degree of strength and endurance required.

FOR THE ARM AND SHOULDER FLEXORS

1 *Chinning the bar or beam:* With the beam above stretch height and hands in overgrasp or undergrasp, bend and stretch the arms. Overgrasp is better when development of the back muscles is required. This exercise is particularly effective for the development of latissimus dorsi, posterior

deltoids, rhomboids and trapezius. Undergrasp with the elbows forward allows more work to be done by the pectorals, biceps and brachialis, as well as the other heaving muscles.

2 *Fall hanging, chinning* (for younger groups): Beam at shoulder height, overgrasp, hands shoulder width apart, body at right angles to the arms, legs and body hanging obliquely under the beam supported by heels and arms, bend arms to raise the chest to the beam (see page 130). Lower the beam to hip height to progress to more difficult work.

3 *Heave jumping* (for younger groups): Beam above stretch height, jump to overgrasp and bend the arms to look over the beam and lower to drop on to the feet again. Repeat with another jump.

4 *Rope climb* (with or without the use of the feet and legs).

5 *Arm curls* (elbow flexor exercise *1*, page 15).

6 *Upright rowing* (shoulder flexor and abductor exercise 2, page 21).

FOR THE ARM AND SHOULDER EXTENSORS
1 *Press-ups:* Front support position with hands shoulder width apart, body and legs in line, supported by the hands and toes. Arm bending and stretching. The exercise may be made easier by resting the hands on the wall-bars or a box. The higher the legs are raised above the hands the greater the work for the arm extensors.

2 *Parallel bar dips* (arm and shoulder extensor exercise 5, page 30).

3 *Jump dips* (for younger groups): Rest the hands on top of the parallel bars, jump to press the arms straight and momentarily support the body between the bars. Lower the feet to the floor and repeat with a jump.

4 *Press behind the neck* (arm and shoulder extensor exercise *10*, page 34).

5 *Two-hand press* (arms and shoulder extensor exercise *11*, page 35).

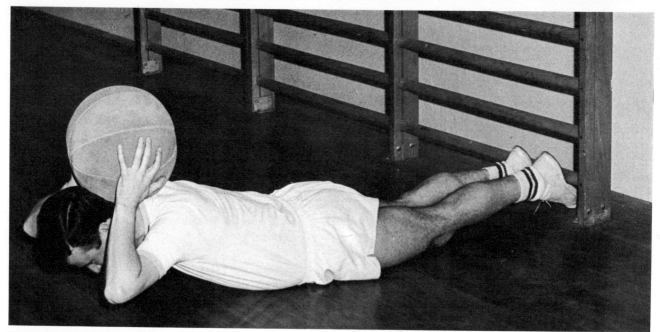

FOR THE DORSAL MUSCLES

1 *Trunk raising backwards with medicine ball:* Prone lying, ball behind the neck, as shown above. Lift the head and chest as high off the floor as possible.

2 *Trunk raising and lowering:* Prone lying across the top section of the box horse, feet held by partner. Trunk raising and lowering.

3 *Heave with bar behind head:* Wide overgrasp of the bar or beam above stretch height. When the body is raised so that the bar passes behind the neck there is a greater dorsal effect (see page 20).

4 *Trunk and arms raising backwards* (dorsal exercise 2, page 50).

FOR THE CHEST MUSCLES

1 *Deep press-ups:* Front support position with hands resting on benches placed shoulder width apart. Bend the arms so that the chest dips between the two benches. Press up again. The wider the benches are and the deeper the chest dips between them, the greater is the load placed on the pectoral muscles.

2 *Rope climb:* The rope-climb activity could be climbing a single rope a given number of times, climbing a single rope without use of the feet, climbing one rope and then travelling sideways to come down the rope at the far end of the group or climbing two parallel vertical ropes without using the feet.

3 *Rope-ladder climb without use of feet.*

4 *Bench press, wide grip* (chest exercise 4, page 58).

FOR THE ABDOMINAL MUSCLES

1 *Trunk curls* (abdominal exercise 1, page 36).

2 *Inclined curls* (abdominal exercise 2, page 38).

3 *Inclined curls with a twist* (abdominal exercise 3, page 39).

4 *Curl sit-ups with legs raised:* Back lying with legs raised almost at right angles and supported against a wall. Sit up to touch the knees with finger tips.

5 *Towel placing on chair:* Front support with shoulders near to chair or box on which rests a rolled towel. On the signal take the towel from chair seat, place it on floor, pick it up with other hand and place on seat. Continue, using alternate hands. Count the number of times towel is placed on seat in 30 seconds.

6 *Double leg lift over towel or vest:* Place vest on floor and sit with legs over the centre of it. Lift both legs together and place on one side of the vest and then on the other, as shown on page 136 and on the right. Count the number of times the heels touch the floor on both sides of the vest in 30 seconds.

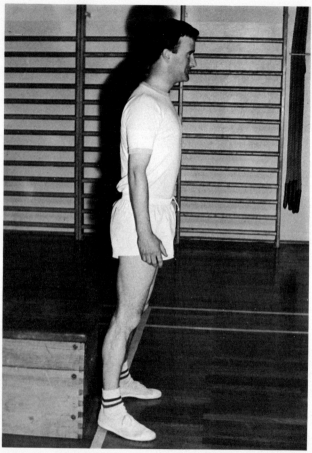

FOR THE LEG MUSCLES

1 *Half squats:* Stand in front of low vaulting box or chair, lower down to a half knees-bend position to touch the top of the box with buttocks and raise up until the legs are almost straight. If the legs are kept slightly bent throughout, the exercise is more taxing because the leg muscles have no opportunity to relax momentarily by allowing the body weight to rest on the joints and ligaments as can occur when the body is balanced in an upright posture (see also page 41).

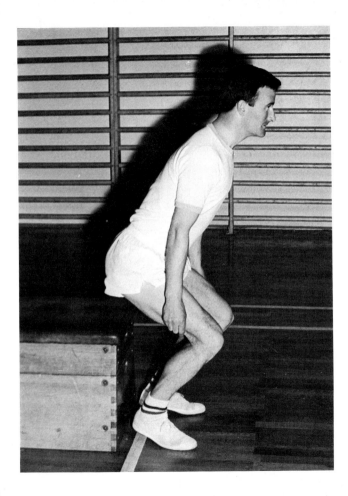

2 *Bench jumps:* Stand astride a low bench holding a medicine ball in each hand. Jump on and off the bench as many times as possible within the prescribed time limit.

3 *Calf raise* (lower leg exercise *1*, page 48).

4 *Shuttle run:* Place two skittles 10 yards apart. Run from one to the other and back again as many times as possible within half a minute (see page 140).

Most of the exercises for general endurance are also leg exercises. They provide vigorous work for the large muscle groups of the body and two-thirds of the muscle mass of the body is in the legs.

1 *Step-ups:* Stand facing a vaulting-box top or bench. Step on to the box with the left foot leading and then step down again, leading with the left foot. Step up and down as many times as possible within 30 and later 60 seconds. Weight may be carried by men who are really fit, as shown on the left.

2 *Bench jumps:* See above in the leg section.

3 *Squat jumps* (knee extensor exercise *5*, page 43 and circuit training exercise *3*, page 123).

4 *Leg thrust:* In the front support position place the left foot forward so that the weight of the body is supported by hands and toes. On the count of one thrust the left foot backwards and bring the right leg forwards under the body. At the count of two change the positions of the legs again.

5 *Vest or towel straddle:* Place a vest or towel on the floor, stand with right foot in front of it and the left foot behind. On the signal to start, change feet positions with a jump (see right and page 143). Count the number of changes made in 30 seconds.

6 *Straddle jumps:* Stand holding a medicine ball under each arm, leap into the air and land with the right foot forwards and the left backwards. On alternate counts of 'one, two, one, two' change the positions of the feet with a jump each time.

6 *Burpees* (circuit training exercise *1*, pages 120 to 121).

7 *The snatch from the 'hang' position:* Stand holding the barbell across the thighs, palms towards the body; then bend the knees and lower the barbell until it almost touches the ground, split the legs in weight lifting style and pull the barbell up to the 'snatch' position at full stretch overhead.

8 *Running:* Either lapping the gymnasium over obstacles or between shuttles for a given number of times within the time limit.

13 Isometric exercises for athletics

MANY COACHES recommend the use of isometric exercises in athletics training programmes. Toni Nett[1] of Germany (DLV-Verbandssportlehrer), for example, advocates the use of a fixed bar or beam to take the place of a barbell so that conventional weight training exercises can be adapted for isometric contractions.

Athletes are advised to exert maximum force against the fixed resistance at the beginning of a weight training type of exercise and again almost at the end of the movement range. The usual routine recommended is to complete no more than three sessions a week with five to eight exercises in each. Obviously not everyone has access to gymnastic equipment but the attraction of isometric exercises lies partly in the fact that they can be adapted for improvised conditions. The lintel of a door-frame, doorways, walls, heavy tables, rubber loops or ropes hooked on the floor, and a partner can all be used to provide the resistance needed to elicit maximum and sustained muscular contractions. To list all possible types of isometric exercises in this book would be confusing and so a selection only has been given as a guide to the athlete who can then improvise and prepare his own exercise schedules.

Apart from strength development there is another important factor recognised in training for athletics and sport today—joint flexibility. Track and field athletes now include a comprehensive mobilising routine in their training programmes. Leading European football teams, Real Madrid and Inter-Milan, take balletic exercises as part of their normal training. Their managers believe that the mobility, agility and general co-ordination developed through balletic springs and jumps improves performance.

It is easy to see that the hurdler and high jumper must be especially supple but not so evident is the need for all athletes to achieve full flexibility of joints and muscles. But physiological research has shown that muscles produce most power immediately after they have been stretched. For example, in javelin throwing, when the arm is pulled back to put the throwing muscles on maximum stretch, the elastic recoil of the muscles gives additional power to the contracting muscles used in the throw.

Strengthen and stretch therefore is the dictum for athletic fitness training today. Suppling exercises keep muscles 'stretchable' whilst isometric and resisted isotonic exercises develop strength.

The successful athlete is the man or woman who can achieve the precise neuro-muscular efficiency to co-ordinate all the physical factors affecting performance—strength, speed and skill. To this physical ability must always be added the quality that makes all the difference between a competent athlete and a champion—motivation, an unquenchable determination to succeed.

Many of the athletic events comprise closely related skills and the basic physical fitness developed for one event will be beneficial in another. Therefore a balanced training schedule of exercises should first be selected from those described on pages 163 to 194. Special exercises and the requirements of different events are discussed below.

Sprinting

Speed depends upon power, the propellant force coming from the thrust of the extending rear leg. The sequence of muscle movements involved is described in greater detail on pages 88 to 89 but here is a brief summary.

The forward motion is a series of propulsive thrusts initiated by the rear leg as it forcibly extends against the ground. The legs are brought alternately under the body to give a moment or two of support in between each forward push. Thus, what actually happens is that the rear leg projects the body weight—say 170 lb—forwards and upwards in the same way as the shot putter's arm projects the shot.

As the sprinter's speed increases, his body is driven a greater distance with each step until top speed is reached and then the stride is at its longest and the ball of the foot strikes the ground only a little behind the body's centre of gravity. During the first twenty paces the sprinter's feet are noticeably behind the body which leans well forward and the stride is not only shorter but more staccato than later in the race when effort is directed from acceleration to the task of moving the limbs rapidly.

From this brief analysis of the sprinter's action it is evident that strength is needed for two purposes:

1 To thrust body weight forward.

2 To move the legs rapidly between each successive thrust.

The main power for the sprinter comes from:

1 *The hip extensors*—gluteus maximus, biceps femoris, semimembranosus, semitendinosus, and the fibres of the abductor magnus that arise from the ischium.

2 *The knee extensors*—quadriceps.

3 *The ankle extensors*—gastrocnemius, soleus, posterior tibial muscle and long flexors of the toes.

Although the greater part of the sprinter's power comes from the hip and knee extensors the final vigorous impetus which lengthens the stride is derived from the ankle extensors and the long flexors of the toes.

The muscle group not yet mentioned, but one that plays a very important part, is the hip flexor group. A high knee lift is essential for sprinters and therefore the psoas and iliacus muscles must be well developed.

So far we have discussed only the propelling muscles, but no muscles can work effectively if the base from which they work is insecure. The muscles which fix the shoulder girdle, back and pelvis must be strong enough to keep the body firm under the vigorous pulling of the prime movers. For example, as the alternate movement of the legs tends to twist the pelvis, the arms must move piston-like across the body in the opposite direction to counteract the twisting and keep the chest square to the front.

Thus, strength training routines for runners must develop strength in the primary muscles of running and also in the fixator groups of the spine, neck and shoulder, which steady the non-moving parts and provide a firm anchorage from which other muscles can work without losing power.

Look closely at a tired runner, his shoulders and neck appear to go limp, the head sinks backwards and begins to pump jerkily with every step. The balance of his body is obviously affected and his style deteriorates so rapidly that his stride diminishes and the driving action is consequently reduced. There must be strength for stability as well as for propulsion. Isometric exercise can develop this strength.

PRE-SEASON TRAINING FOR SPRINTERS

Opinions vary as to the amount of pre-season strength training needed by sprinters but the minimum appears to be four weeks. Some British coaches favour a longer programme, but clearly the time depends upon the athlete's physique and the intensity of the exercise taken. Generally, an athlete who trains four times a week using isotonic and isometric exercise should have built adequate strength within four to six weeks.

An additional advantage of pre-season training is that it

appears to reduce the risk of injuries early in the season.

At this point the fact must be stressed that no matter how much an athlete trains for strength, running is still the most important exercise for track events and practice of throws and jumps the principal training for field events.

ISOMETRIC EXERCISES FOR SPRINTERS

1 Feet flat on the floor, arms upwards bent beneath beam or bar, knees bent. Press upwards as if trying to straighten the legs during the squat or knee bending and stretching exercise. This exercise can also be done in a doorway with knees bent and hands pressing upwards on the lintel. In order to develop the quadriceps muscles thoroughly, practise the exercise with beam at different heights so that knees are bent at forty-five, ninety and one hundred and forty degrees. Different parts of the quadriceps work more effectively during different stages of the leg extension. If a fixed beam is not available use a bench or box in a doorway to alter the angle of the knee.

2 Sit on a chair, place hands on the seat below thighs and press the back of the heels against the chair leg. This exercise develops strength in the knee flexor muscles at the back of the legs. The exercise can also be done sitting on top of a gymnastic box horse.

3 A good knee lift is important in sprinting. The leg is lifted by the hip flexor muscles, psoas or iliacus. Stand

facing vaulting box, body leaning forward. Raise knee as high as possible with partner providing resistance as shown above.

146

4 Stand under a fixed bar or beam with a pad across the shoulders, legs straight. Try to lift the heels from the ground whilst pressing against the bar.

5 As an alternative to exercise 4, stand in a doorway with arms straight and hands flat against the lintel as shown on the left. Adjust the leg positions backwards if you are tall so that the body and legs are straight in one line. By contracting the calf muscle try to rise on to the toes.

6 Stand on the left leg, body leaning forward, hands holding a doorway or wall-bar, right knee raised, facing partner who clasps his hands behind and above the right knee. By tightening the buttock muscles try to draw the right leg backwards. Change legs.

7 Stand with one leg raised so that thigh is parallel to floor and foot against door jamb. Press outwards with raised foot to feel quadriceps, particularly vastus medialis, contracting strongly (see page 148).

8 Sit with legs straight, body leaning slightly backwards and arms propping the body. Press outwards with feet against door jambs. In this exercise the gluteus minimus and medius work strongly to abduct the legs. These are the muscles which tilt the pelvis to one side thus lifting the opposite leg clear of the ground to allow a free swing through in running and walking. The development of these muscles

is essential for efficient style in running—weak muscles make running look like an exaggerated duck-like waddle.

Hurdling

The hurdler's start and his steps in between hurdles are identical to those of the sprinter. Training too is very similar: the same muscle groups provide the power and the speed. But there is one feature of hurdle training which needs more emphasis on suppling exercises. The beginner must work hard to achieve maximum flexibility of the hips and thighs. Success in the event cannot be achieved without this.

ISOMETRIC EXERCISES FOR HURDLERS

The sprinters' exercises *1* to *6* are strongly recommended together with the additional ones described below:

1 Stand with leading leg raised straight and with the heel resting on a beam at hurdle height. Press down strongly. This exercise strengthens the muscles used in the snapping down action of the leg.

2 From the back-lying position, knees bent, raise the body upwards to bring the chin towards the knees. A training partner should hold the legs down with one hand and apply resistance to the chest as it is lifted upwards (see page 149). This exercise strengthens the muscles stabilising the pelvis and the hip flexor muscles used in the knee lift.

Middle- and long-distance running

Basically there is no significant difference between the movements of the sprinter and those of the longer distance runner. A. G. K. Brown in his chapter on 'Sprinting'[2] writes, 'Such differences as there are—in stride length, speed and range of movement of limbs, position of the trunk and action of the shoulders—can be explained as the natural result of difference of effort and speed and not as the result of trying to run in a different way.' In longer races the body lean is not as great, the pace more rhythmical and the arm action more in front of the body, but the running form is fundamentally the same as in sprinting. The distinctive feature between sprinting and long-distance running is primarily that the former need not consider 'oxygen debt' and the recovery factor during a race, whereas it is not until the final sprint for the tape that the long-distance runner can pour full effort into his race.

Training for the half-mile and upwards must therefore develop speed with stamina. We know that speed involves power which depends upon strength.

Coaches of successful international runners vary in their opinions about training methods, but the aim in winter training is the same—to produce physical and mental toughness, a combination of strength, stamina and the compelling inner motivation that enables an athlete to ignore during a race the symptons of distress and to accept pain as something to be met and run through. While

Cerutty believes in running up sandhills and weight lifting, Stampfl sticks mainly to track interval running. Each athlete, according to his body build and temperament, must make his own decision and have faith in his coach.

However, there is still general agreement that middle- and long-distance runners must be strong and because isometric exercises take so little time to produce marked gains in strength—a minute a day—three sessions a week are bound to be beneficial to the athlete who has little time and wants to get fit quickly.

ISOMETRIC EXERCISES FOR MIDDLE- AND LONG-DISTANCE RUNNERS

Exercises *1*, *4* and *8* of exercises for sprinters are recommended. The 'sit-up' exercise (*8*) is particularly beneficial to runners because it develops the abdominal muscles which stabilise the pelvis, thereby reducing fatigue in running, and strengthens the hip flexor muscles used in the high knee lift.

1 Stand with one knee raised under a beam or bar. Place a folded towel as a pad on the knee. Press upwards with the raised leg against the beam. Change leg positions. This exercise develops strength in the psoas and iliacus muscles which flex the hip and provide the power for the high knee lift.

2 Back lying with one knee slightly raised. Partner holds the raised foot whilst the subject tries to raise his knee. The

partner should apply resistance at several stages of the movement.

3 Hang from the top wall-bar, facing the wall, with one leg bent backwards at the knee. A partner presses down whilst the subject strives to maintain the position.

Jumping

The force required to project the body upwards or forwards is directly proportional to body weight. (The heavier you are the more power is needed. Excess fat is an obvious handicap.) The muscles providing jumping power are:

1 *The hip extensors* of the take-off leg—gluteals.
2 *The knee extensors*—quadriceps.
3 *The ankle flexors* in the calf-gastrocnemius and soleus.
4 *The flexor muscles of the foot*—tibialis posticus and long flexors of the toes.

But muscles never work in isolation. Whilst the prime movers are effecting the required movement other muscles work to fix points of origin and insertion, prevent unwanted movement in other joints and control the force and direction of the power released. For example, in the high jump the pelvis is firmly fixed by contracted abdominals as the leg is swung upwards. In order to maintain a balanced and constantly changing pattern of posture as the body passes over the bar the spine, neck and head have to be stabilised.

Long jumpers also have to maintain a balanced poise during flight if maximum distance and an efficient landing is to be achieved.

Pole vaulters need not only power for the upward spring but also strength in the arm, shoulder and abdominal muscles to heave and swing higher up the pole and over the bar.

The isometric exercises listed below will develop the leg power for take-off and the general strength needed for postural stability. In addition to strength and power another factor of fitness needs developing—endurance. High-jump and pole-vault events are often very long and drawn out. Fatigue often determines whether or not peak performance can be produced. Training for these events therefore should include activities and specific exercises to develop stamina.

ISOMETRIC EXERCISES FOR JUMPERS AND POLE VAULTERS

Exercises *1*, *4* and *8* of exercises for sprinters are strongly recommended for jumpers and pole vaulters.

SPECIAL EXERCISES FOR HIGH JUMPERS

1 Half lie on top of a vaulting box, one leg on the top, the swinging leg dangling as on page 152. Try to raise this leg against a training partner's resistance.

2 Sit on a box top with knee slightly bent and foot under a fixed bar or held by a partner. Exert maximum pressure against the bar as though trying to straighten the leg.

3 Hang from a beam with one foot flat on the floor and the other trailing behind, toe just touching the floor. A partner holds the ankle of the trailing leg, whilst the subject tries to swing the leg through.

ADDITIONAL EXERCISE FOR LONG JUMPERS

1 With arms straight supporting the body on parallel bars or a strong armchair, raise the legs to a right-angle position at the hips. A partner applies a gentle pressure downwards on the ankles. This exercise is particularly valuable to long jumpers as it develops strength in the abdominal and hip flexor muscles used to keep the legs high and straight during the last phase of the jump. When the legs drop too soon contact with the ground is made earlier and valuable inches lost.

ADDITIONAL EXERCISES FOR POLE VAULTERS

1 Hang from the top wall-bar, knees raised, arms straight. A training partner holds the ankles whilst the subject tries to curl his body and legs upwards as if trying to tuck them under the top wall-bar.

2 Hang from a rope with hands in positions corresponding to the grip on the wall-bar. A partner holds the ankles whilst the subject tries to heave his body upwards.

Throwing

For an athlete to succeed in throwing events he needs exceptional strength in the arm and shoulder muscles coupled with a high degree of neuro-muscular co-ordination. The power generated in the whole body during the preliminary swings or run-up must be unleashed with maximum efficiency at precisely the right moment. Skill training must, therefore, go hand-in-hand with training for strength. Isometric exercises recommended for the throwing events are described below.

PUTTING THE SHOT

1 With a fixed bar or beam across the back of the shoulders and the body in the forward lunge position, right foot forward, push backwards as if trying to regain the standing position. Insert a towel pad between the spine and the bar or beam.

2 Lie under a fixed bar or beam. Push upwards immediately above the shoulders. Adjust the beam so that the arm

extensors work with the elbows bent and with them almost straight.

3 Lie on an inclined bench with a stick or barbell bar across the chest. Partner applies resistance at different stages of the arm thrust. The position on the inclined bench is recommended because it coincides better with the angle adopted in the actual shot-putting technique.

4 Place the body in the position for a standing throw under a fixed beam or bar. Exert utmost pressure against the beam.

THROWING THE DISCUS

1 Stand feet astride, back of shoulders against a beam a little below shoulder height. Raise arms sideways and grasp beam, palms forward, knees slightly bent. Try to rotate from the waist whilst the feet and shoulders remain fixed.

2 Stand with left foot forward as in the position for a standing throw and with the right arm backwards so that the hand is behind a vaulting box, or heavy piece of furniture. Using the arm and shoulder muscles only, push hard against the resistance.

3 Stand leaning forwards with arms wide and straight, palms against a wall. Press hard as if to push the hands through the wall.

THROWING THE JAVELIN

1 Partners face each other holding a pole above the head with both hands, as shown on page 155. One partner pushes whilst the other provides resistance for the trunk flexor and the arm and shoulder muscles used in the throwing actions.

2 In the throwing position a partner holds the thrower's hand at various stages of the movement and offers sufficient resistance to cause the thrower to elicit maximum effort to achieve any movement of his throwing arm. The resistance may be increased at different phases of the action.

3 Hold a stick with both hands above the head so that one end presses against the wall. Exert pressure with the arms and trunk at all stages of the throwing action.

4 Sit on a vaulting-box top and hold ropes in both hands with arms outstretched above and behind the head. The ends of the ropes should be attached to a low rung of the wall-bars or to a floor ring. Pull hard with the arms and use the abdominal muscles to try and flex the trunk forwards. Strong rubber rings attached to the ropes will allow a little movement and ensure that maximum muscle contraction is elicited to maintain the final position.

5 Stand with hands above the head, fingers linked, palms forward, elbows slightly forward of the face and back resting

against the wall. A partner attempts to push the elbows back whilst the thrower resists.

6 Back lying on a long vaulting box with arms outstretched overhead and hands pressing against a fixed beam or bar. Feet should be fixed in the wall-bars or held by a partner. Push upwards with both hands.

7 Stand back to back with a partner, elbows linked, feet astride. Twist first to the left and then to the right (partners are then trying to twist in opposite directions). (See page 185.)

THROWING THE HAMMER

1 Kneel on a rubber mat with legs about 12 inches apart, arms sideways resting behind and over a fixed bar or beam. Try to turn the trunk first to the left and then to the right.

2 With the beam at slightly below shoulder height and knees slightly bent attempt the same trunk rotation movements.

3 Stand in the position for beginning a standing throw. Partner holds on to hands which are in position for gripping the hammer handle. Pull against partner exerting resistance at various stages of the turn (see page 156).

4 Stand with arms straight and crossed at shoulder height in front of the body. A partner presses against the sides of the thrower's wrists as he tries to uncross his arms.

5 Back flat against the wall, knees bent, feet 18 inches from the wall and hands on knees. Push backwards against the wall using the thigh muscles.

6 In the standing throw position hold a fixed bar, beam or wall-bar. Attempt to turn whilst still holding the bar.

REFERENCES
1 Toni Nett, *Leichtathletisches Muskeltraining* (Bartels and Wernitz, Berlin).
2 A. G. K. Brown, 'Sprinting', Chapter 1 of *Athletics*, ed. by G. F. D. Pearson (Nelson).

14 Isometric exercises for improving sports performance

FOR IMPROVING GRIP

1 Hold a broomstick horizontally with hands shoulder width apart. Grip hard and then try to twist the handle. Change the direction in which the hands are twisting.

2 Fold a towel into a roll so that your hand can just curl round it. Carry out the same twisting movement as above.

3 Rest both elbows, body width apart, on a table or desk top, finger-tips against each other (see right). Press hard, using the finger flexor muscles only, and gradually force the palms of the hand apart keeping the fingers straight.

4 Place one hand over and around the opposite fist so that the palm of the gripping hand touches the back of the other. Squeeze hard as if trying to compress the fist.

FOR DEVELOPING WRIST STRENGTH

Strength in the muscles which move or lock the wrist is important in golf, squash, badminton and tennis. All the exercises described below can be done at any time of the day and are most effective in developing the strength required.

1 Bend the wrist inwards as far as possible and place the other hand on top, as shown on the right. Try to straighten the wrist until it is in line with the forearm. Allow a little movement to take place so that the wrist extensor muscles can work at different phases of extension movement.

2 Place the right elbow on the table with the hand palm uppermost and bent backwards towards the shoulder. Place the left hand upon the right. Try to straighten the right wrist. Apply pressure at different stages of the flexion movement.

FOR POWER IN THE GOLF SWING

The ideal golf swing is one in which a pattern of perfect timing is established so that all the available power is utilised in proper sequence and at exactly the right moment. It is a highly complicated skill, but it has been analysed by kinesiologists using slow-motion film so that coaching points can be more easily understood. Professors Morehouse and Cooper of California University write[1] that in the golf swing 'the hips move forward first, followed in order by a

twist of the trunk, a rotation of the shoulders, a sweep of the arms and a whip of the wrists. These actions are not hurried but surge after one another'. How do we start to add power to the swing once good timing has been established? The arm sweep contributes more force than the rotation of the shoulders and therefore strength in the deltoid muscle will provide the power to be utilised in the perfectly timed swing. Remember that control must never be sacrificed for power. The two exercises described below will develop strong deltoid muscles.

1 Stand with right arm forward and palm pressing against a piece of heavy furniture or door jamb. Place the fingers and thumb of the left hand around the right wrist, as shown on the right. Keeping the left arm as straight as possible, pull hard to try and draw the right arm forward.

2 Stand with feet astride, and backs of both fists touching the door jambs. Press hard against the woodwork. This exercise develops the deltoid muscles and extensors of the wrist.

FOR THE POWERFUL FOREHAND DRIVE IN TENNIS

The power for this stroke comes from contraction of the coraco-brachialis, the pectoralis major, the biceps and the frontal fibres of the deltoid muscle. Just before the racket meets the ball the wrist flexor muscles bring the racket head sharply forward so that the handle and forearm are in line.

At this point of impact the wrist should be firmly locked to ensure fullest utilisation of the power derived from the contracting muscles and momentum.

The oblique abdominal muscles which rotate the trunk during the drive add power to the stroke. In the backhand strokes the opposite group of oblique muscles work.

Once good style and timing has been established, increased strength will improve performance. The following isometric exercises are recommended in addition to a general strengthening routine.

1 Kneel between two chairs, place one hand flat on each seat so that the arms are bent and the chest is down below the hands. Press hard on to the chair seats as if performing press-ups.

2 Stand with left hand grasping the edge of a door at eye-level, place the right hand on the door at hip height so that the right arm is almost straight. Press hard with the right hand whilst offering resistance with pressure from the left, as shown on the right. Try also to use the trunk rotator muscles in the effort to bring the right arm forward.

FOR STRENGTHENING THE TENNIS SERVE

The forceful serve derives its power from the triceps, the pectorals and the middle fibres of the deltoid muscle, assisted by the serratus anterior. To obtain maximum force at the point of impact the serving arm should be fully

extended. A good exercise for developing strength in the main muscles used in serving is:

1 Stand with left foot forward in a doorway, the right arm straight above the head slightly to the side and the palm of the hand against the wall and press hard. Give a series of vigorous presses (as if trying to push a hole in the wall) after you have held the first contraction for ten seconds.

Exercises 3 to 7, designed for javelin throwers, are also useful in developing strength in the muscles used in tennis serving.

THE SMASH (BADMINTON, SQUASH, TENNIS AND VOLLEY BALL)

A winning smash begins with a powerful extension of the legs followed by a strike at the peak of the jump. It is a skill demanding a very high degree of neuro-muscular co-ordination. Judgement of the direction and the speed of the falling ball is made without conscious thought and then the leg muscles are stimulated, entirely by reflex, to project the body upwards so that the stroke can be made from the most effective position.

Strong leg muscles provide the power which enables the good player to bring off more successful shots than an equally skilled opponent who is unable to jump as high because his muscles are weaker. (See also page 151, 'Jumping'.)

The upward thrust is given to the body by the hip, knee and ankle extensor muscles assisted by the long flexors of the toes. Special exercises to develop these muscles are listed below.

1 Stand with your back against the woodwork of a doorway, right leg raised to waist height and ball of the foot (bare) against the opposite woodwork. Press downwards and outwards. Feel the muscles of thigh and calf contracting. Support your body by resting the right hand against the door jamb. Change legs and hands.

2 Sit with chair against a wall. Raise your heels and press downwards and outwards on the floor with balls of your feet. Place your hands on your thighs just above and towards the inside of the knees and feel the quadriceps muscles contracting. Do the exercise in bare feet or in non-skid shoes.

The exercises on page 153 in the athletics chapter are also recommended for developing the muscles used in jumping.

REFERENCE
1 L. E. Morehouse and J. M. Cooper, *Kinesiology* (The C. V. Mosby Company, St Louis).

15 Isometric exercises for the major muscle groups

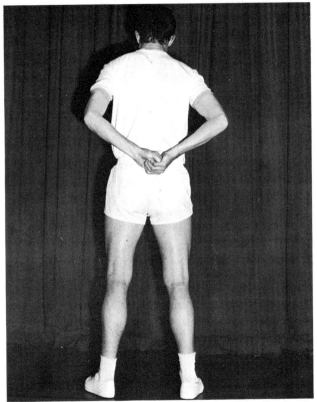

Note: All these exercises are suitable for both men and women. Maintain the effort for 10 seconds.

FOR THE ARM AND SHOULDER MUSCLES

1 Lie face down, hands flat on the floor by the hips and fingers pointing towards feet. Press downwards with the arms, trying to bend the elbows and lift head and shoulders off the floor.

2 Back lying, arms straight by the sides, palms flat on the floor. Press downwards with hands and arms. Heels, hands and head maintain contact with the floor whilst pressure of the hands lifts the back and pelvis.

3 Place the left hand on top of the right fist. Try to bend the right arm towards the shoulder whilst pressing downwards with the left. Change hands.

4 With arms behind the back, place the right fist in the left hand, as shown above. Try to extend the right arm whilst opposing the movement with the left.

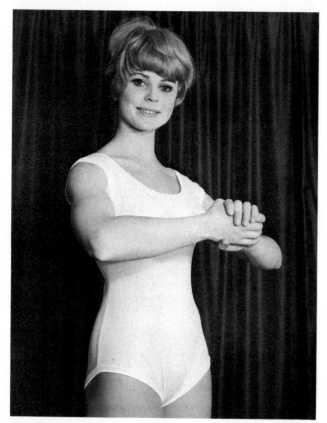

5 With arms half bent across the chest, place one hand in the other, as shown above. Press together.

6 Link the hands across the chest and pull outwards as strongly as possible, as shown above.

7 Grasp a broomstick, wall-bar or racket handle. Twist the hands in opposite directions.

8 Stand with arms midway upwards, sides of hands against sides of doorway, as shown on the left. Press outwards.

FOR THE NECK MUSCLES

1 Place the palm of the left hand against the left temple. Try to bend and turn the head towards the left shoulder. Place right hand to right temple and repeat.

2 Link the hands behind the head and press the head firmly backwards, as shown on the left. When doing this exercise do not exert maximum force with the arm and shoulder muscles to pull the head forward. Rather use them to prevent the head from moving backwards.

3 Place the fingers and palm of the right hand against the right cheek. Keeping the chin level, try to turn the head to the right.

FOR THE DORSAL MUSCLES

1 Back lying, arms sideways, elbows bent at ninety degrees to the floor. Keeping the back of the head and seat in contact with the floor, press strongly downwards with the elbows. Allow the back and shoulders to be lifted a little clear of the floor but avoid hollowing of the back through the employment of other muscle groups (see page 167).

2 Back lying, knees raised, feet flat on the floor, arms overhead, straight but relaxed with fingers lightly curled and knuckles resting on the ground. Tighten the dorsal muscles to pull the coccyx towards the back of the head and hollow the back in the lumbar region. This exercise should be followed by a strong abdominal exercise such as the one in the back-lying position, no. *1* in the abdominal group.

3 Stand feet astride, arms forward with palms of hands flat on ledge or furniture at shoulder height. Press downwards.

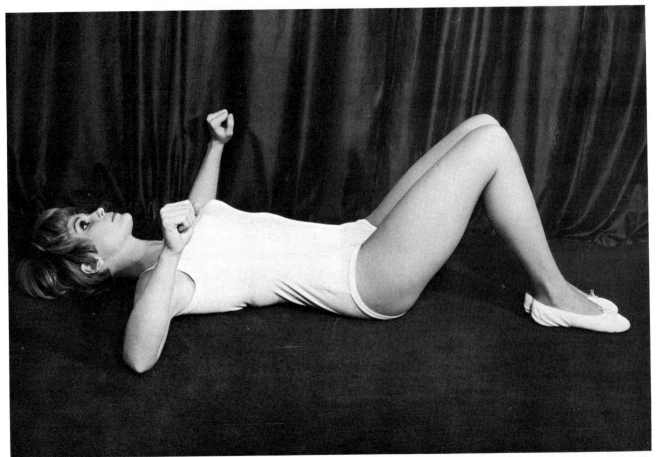

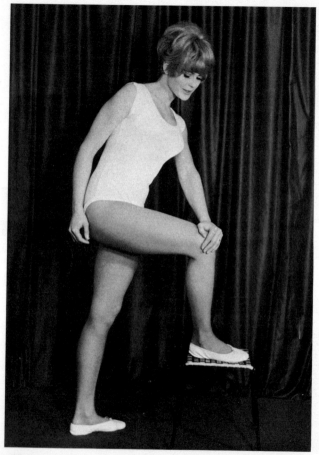

FOR THE CHEST MUSCLES

1 Sit with feet and knees 18 inches apart. Lean forward, placing the hands to the side and slightly on top of the knee joints. Press inwards and downwards.

2 Stand with right foot on a chair and place the left hand on the inside of the right knee, press outwards and downwards with hand while resisting with knee as shown on the left. The abdominal muscles are then brought more into contraction as well as the pectoral muscles. Change hand and knee positions.

3 Sit with arms slightly bent above the head. Place the left fist in the right hand. Press forwards and downwards with the right hand whilst resisting with the left.

4 Stand with hands wide apart on top of a vaulting horse, as shown above, or grasping the wall-bars. Push both arms firmly inwards.

5 Stand facing a wall, feet 20 inches away from it with arms sideways at shoulder height and bent at the elbows, palms of the hands against the wall. Keeping the chest away from the wall, press inwards and forwards as though trying to push the hands through the wall to bring the arms together.

FOR THE ABDOMINAL MUSCLES

1 Back lying, knees raised and feet flat on the floor, arms midway upwards, straight but relaxed, with fingers lightly curled and knuckles resting on the ground. Pull the pubis towards the chest and flatten the back as much as possible.

2 With body bent forward and knees slightly bent place hands on knees, thumbs innermost. Press downwards with the whole body as strongly as possible. Try to feel the abdominal muscles pulling the body downwards.

3 Sit on the floor or bed with one knee raised and place both hands on the knee, as shown on the right. Press downwards to force the knee away from the body and at the same time draw the knee towards the chest. Change legs.

4 Sit well back on a bench or chair with legs raised straight and hands placed above the knees. Press downwards with the hands whilst trying to raise the thighs towards the chest.

5 *Abdominal retraction:* Stand with the upper part of the body leaning forward at the hips and hands on the front of the thighs. Breathe out forcibly and then try to pull your stomach muscles backwards towards the spine and upwards under the rib cage making a dome-like hollow, as shown on the right.

6 Stand with knees half bent, body leaning slightly forward and hands on knees, thumbs on the inside. From this semi-squat position push down on to the knees as hard as possible.

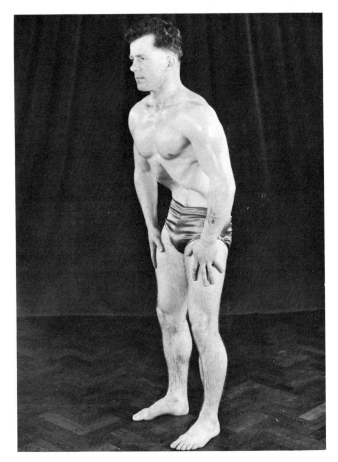

7 Sitting, knees raised, place hands on knees and push forward with the arms as if trying to straighten the knees, as shown below.

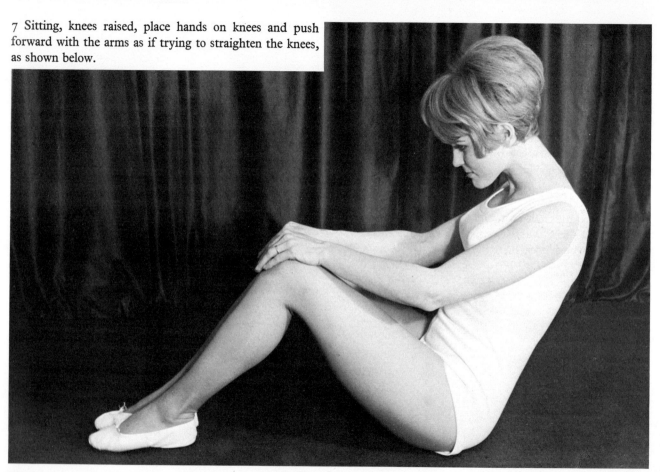

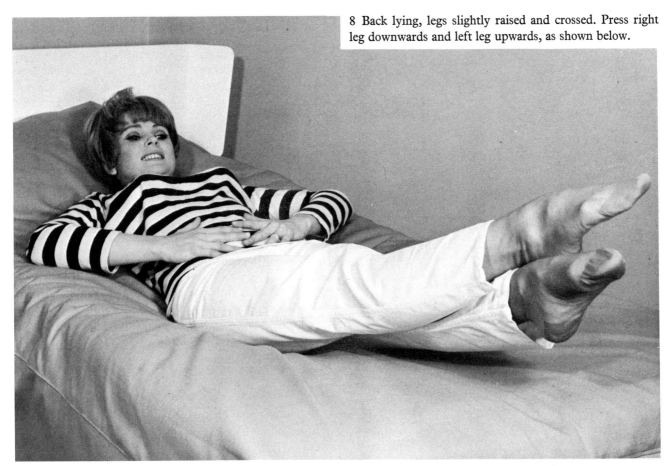

8 Back lying, legs slightly raised and crossed. Press right leg downwards and left leg upwards, as shown below.

FOR THE LEG MUSCLES

1 Stand back to a wall with heels about 10 inches from it, bend the knees so that they are slightly in front of the toes, thighs almost parallel to the floor as shown on the left. Press forwards with the feet. This exercise should be done on a non-slippery floor with gym shoes that grip, or in bare feet.

2 Stand in the same position as above but raise the heels as high as possible and lower the seat farther down. Maintain the position for 10 seconds.

3 Sit with knees slightly bent and about 18 inches apart. Lean forward, place the hands on the inside of the knees with arms slightly bent. Press inwards with the legs and outwards and backwards with the arms. This exercise also strengthens the abdominal muscles.

4 Half lie with one knee bent. Loop towel under instep. Press leg straight whilst pulling towel against foot (see page 175).

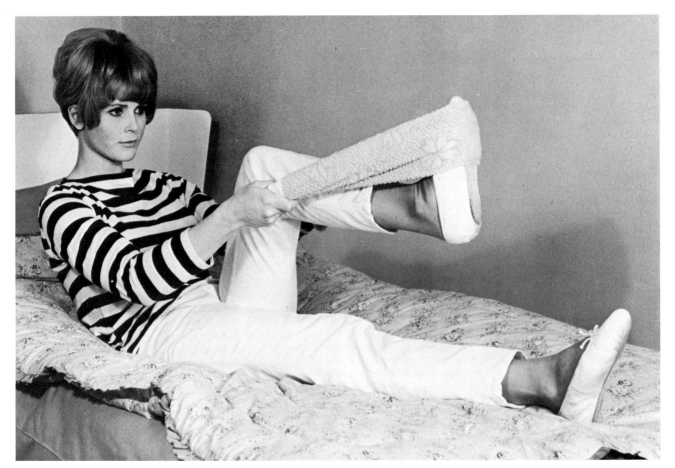

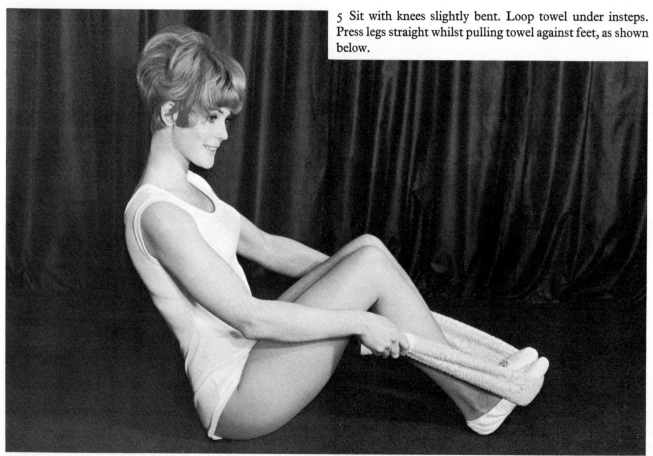

5 Sit with knees slightly bent. Loop towel under insteps. Press legs straight whilst pulling towel against feet, as shown below.

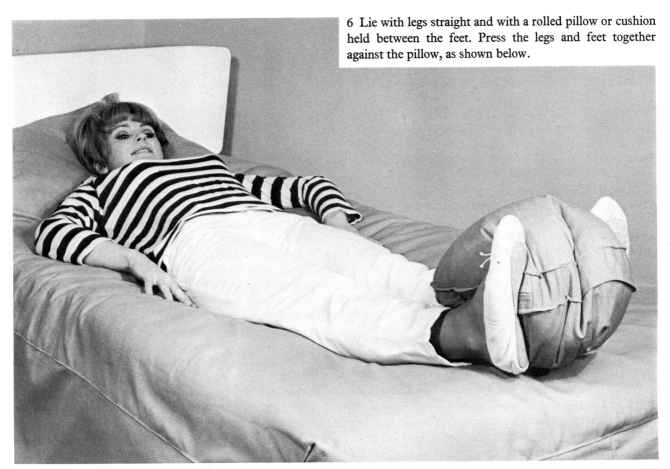

6 Lie with legs straight and with a rolled pillow or cushion held between the feet. Press the legs and feet together against the pillow, as shown below.

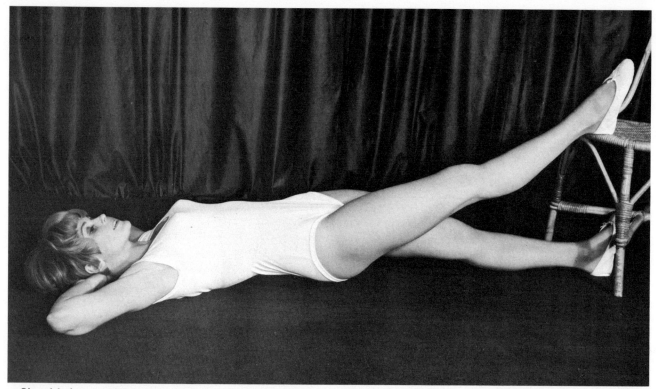

7 Sit with legs straight, body leaning slightly backwards and arms propping the body. Press outwards with the feet against the door jambs. (See exercises for sprinters on page 146 for particular value of this exercise.)

8 Back lying with one leg raised and heel resting on a chair or vaulting-box top, as shown above. Press downwards with the raised leg to lift the buttocks clear of the ground. A good exercise for the hip extensor muscles.

16 Partner isometric exercises

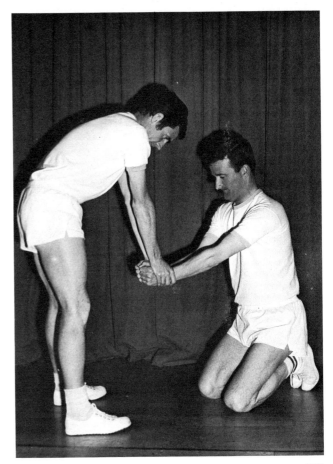

FOR THE ARM AND SHOULDER MUSCLES

1 *Arms pressing upwards:* Stand facing partner with arms forward, slightly below shoulder level. No. 2 places his hands on top of no. 1's fists. The arms of no. 1 should be slightly bent at the elbow to strengthen the mechanical position of the joint and to allow a greater force to be exerted upwards. No. 1 presses upwards whilst no. 2 holds the partner's arms down.

2 *Arms pressing outwards:* No. 1 kneel-sitting with arms forward and slightly bent at the elbow. No. 2, stooping, places his hands outside no. 1's fists, and presses inwards as no. 1 presses outwards, as shown on the right.

3 *Elbow raising upwards:* No. 1 kneel-sitting, arms bent across the chest. No. 2 stands behind no. 1 with hands placed on top of the elbows. No. 1 presses upwards as no. 2 resists.

4 *Elbow pressing backwards:* No. 1 adopts a forward-lean position with knees slightly bent and back straight. His arms are bent across the chest, elbows level with the shoulders. No. 2, standing by the side of, and slightly behind, no. 1, places the palms of his hands over no. 1's elbows. No. 1 presses backwards to lift his elbows away from the floor and to draw the shoulder blades together whilst no. 2 resists.

5 *Arm bending:* No. 1 stands with arms bent and hands behind his neck but without fingers being interlocked. No. 2 stands behind no. 1 and grasps the wrists, as shown on the left. No. 2 pushes upwards to force the hands apart whilst no. 1 tries to keep them together.

6 *One-hand wrestle:* Partners prone lying, facing each other with one hand forward, elbows bent and in line. Hands grasp, palm to palm. Each tries to force his partner's hand over backwards to touch the ground.

7 *Press-ups against resistance:* No. 1 in front-support position with arms half bent. No. 2 stands alongside no. 1's body and places his hands flat on his back. No. 1 tries to straighten his arms, pushing hard against his partner's resistance (see page 181).

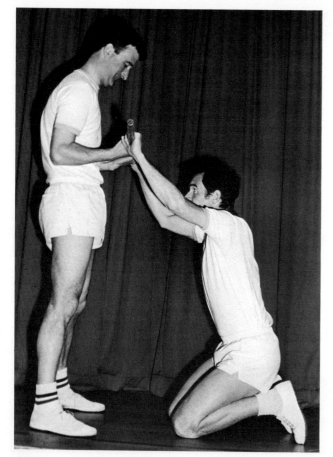

8 *Arm curls:* No. 1 stands with arms half bent, holding a bar or broom handle. No. 2 kneels and grasps broom handle, as shown on the left. No. 1 tries to bend his arms upwards whilst no. 2 exerts sufficient resistance to prevent the completion of the movement.

FOR THE DORSAL MUSCLES

1 *Head pressing backwards:* No. 1 kneels, with head braced firmly back against gentle pressure of no. 2's hands placed on top of head (see page 183). Whilst in this position also exercise the neck flexor muscles by placing hands beneath forehead as shown on page 184 and providing resistance to neck flexion.

2 *Back to back, sideways wrestle:* Stand back to back with elbows interlocked. Partners try to bend first to the left and then to the right as indicated by the instructor (no. 1's 'left' is, of course, no. 2's 'right').

3 *Back to back, trunk turning:* Partners stand back to back as above and try to turn the trunk to the left and then to the right against each other's efforts, as shown on the right. This exercise can also be done in the astride long-sitting position.

4 *Trunk raising backwards against resistance:* No. 1 prone lying, hands behind the head. No. 2 kneels astride and rests both hands on no. 1's shoulders. He should allow no. 1 to raise his chest off the ground and then exert enough resistance to force no. 1 to abandon the position after about 10 seconds.

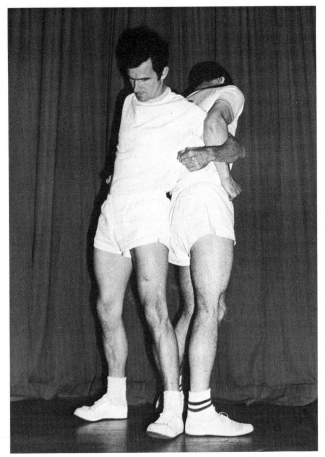

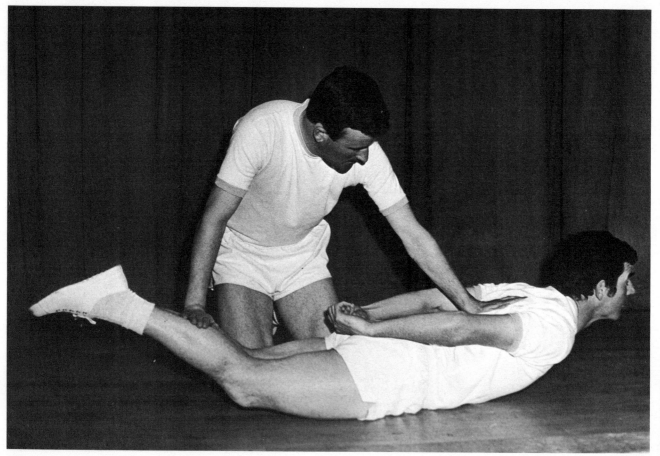

5 *Trunk and legs raising backwards:* No. 1 prone lying, hands behind back, whilst no. 2 provides resistance against the back and the legs as shown on page 186. No. 1 raises his chest and legs off the floor and no. 2 applies sufficient opposition to make no. 1 give up the attempt after 10 seconds.

1 *Arms pressing inwards:* No. 1 stands with arms directly forward, slightly bent at the elbows and forearms at shoulder height. No. 2 places his hands over the top of, and inside no. 1's and presses outwards as no. 1 tries to bring his arms together.

2 *Single arm pushing forward:* No. 1 stands with left leg advanced, right arm forward at shoulder height, slightly bent, and hand resting flat against no. 2's hand which is bent upwards so that the palm of the hand is level with his shoulder and braced against his chest. No. 1 pushes forward trying to straighten his arm and thrust no. 2 away whilst no. 2 leans his body weight against the force.

3 *Straight arm pushing forward:* Partners stand in the same position as described above except that no. 1's arm is straight. He then pushes hard to bring his shoulder forward as far as possible.

4 *Straight arm pullovers:* The name of the exercise is a well-known weight training term. No. 1 in back-lying position on a bench, with his feet and knees astride, arms stretched overhead as in the weight training exercise on page 55. No. 2 kneels and holds no. 1's wrists. No. 1 tries to raise his arms forwards and upwards. For a second attempt at this exercise the arms should be fixed at a point higher from the floor than they were at first.

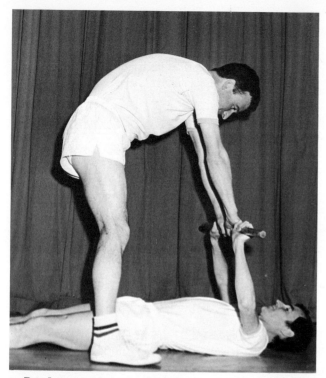

5 *Bench press:* No. 1 back lying on a bench or the floor, arms slightly bent and hands grasping bar or broom handle, as shown above. No. 2, standing astride no. 1, places his hands over the bar to resist when no. 1 tries to straighten his arms.

FOR THE ABDOMINAL MUSCLES

1 *Trunk curls from sitting:* No. 1 sits on the floor with knees raised, and hands lightly resting on them to maintain starting position. No. 2 stands behind and places his hands against no. 1's forehead. No. 1 tries to pull his head and trunk down towards his knees (without using his hands). No. 2 applies just enough resistance to allow a little movement.

2 *Trunk raising from sitting:* No. 1 half lying with hands behind the head and body inclined backwards at forty-five degrees to the floor. No. 2 places his right hand over no. 1's feet and his left hand against no. 1's chest, as shown on page 189. No. 1 tries to sit up against the resistance.

3 *Trunk curls maintained against resistance:* In this exercise, no. 1 adopts the trunk curl position first with feet under wallbars or with legs held by no. 2. No. 2 applies pressure to the forehead with the palm of his hand. No. 1 tries to maintain his position but no. 2 must try to make his partner give way after 10 seconds.

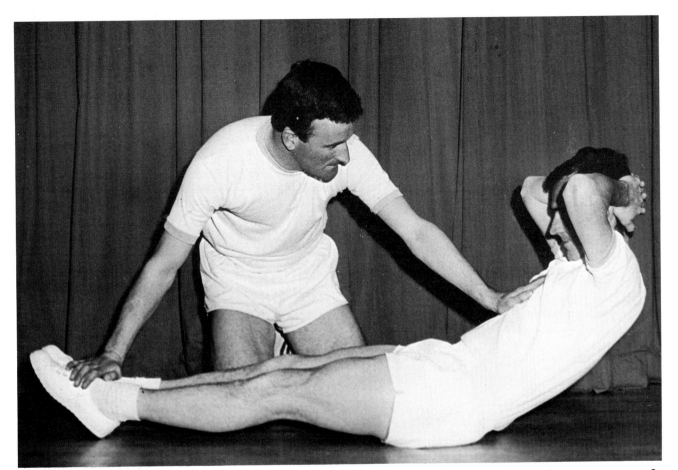

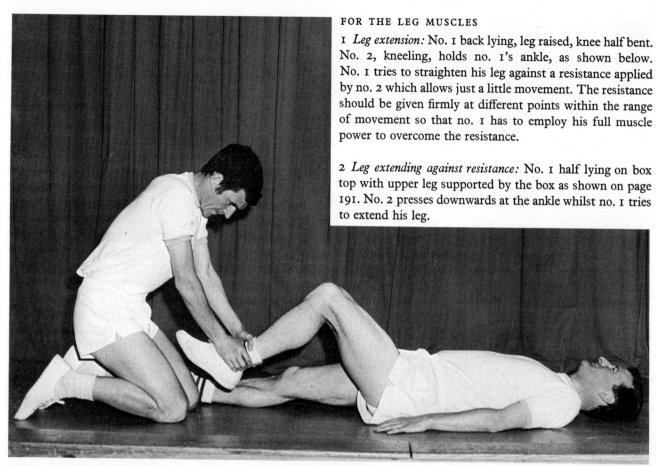

FOR THE LEG MUSCLES

1 *Leg extension:* No. 1 back lying, leg raised, knee half bent. No. 2, kneeling, holds no. 1's ankle, as shown below. No. 1 tries to straighten his leg against a resistance applied by no. 2 which allows just a little movement. The resistance should be given firmly at different points within the range of movement so that no. 1 has to employ his full muscle power to overcome the resistance.

2 *Leg extending against resistance:* No. 1 half lying on box top with upper leg supported by the box as shown on page 191. No. 2 presses downwards at the ankle whilst no. 1 tries to extend his leg.

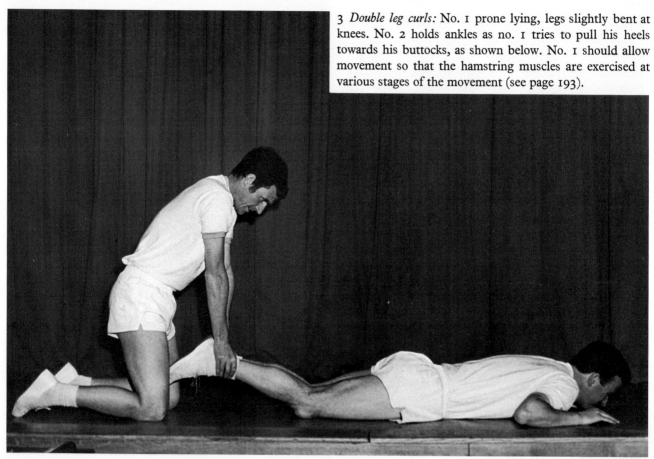

3 *Double leg curls:* No. 1 prone lying, legs slightly bent at knees. No. 2 holds ankles as no. 1 tries to pull his heels towards his buttocks, as shown below. No. 1 should allow movement so that the hamstring muscles are exercised at various stages of the movement (see page 193).

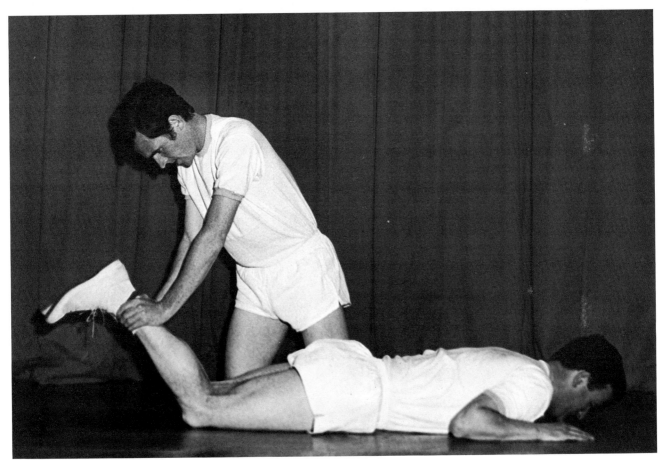

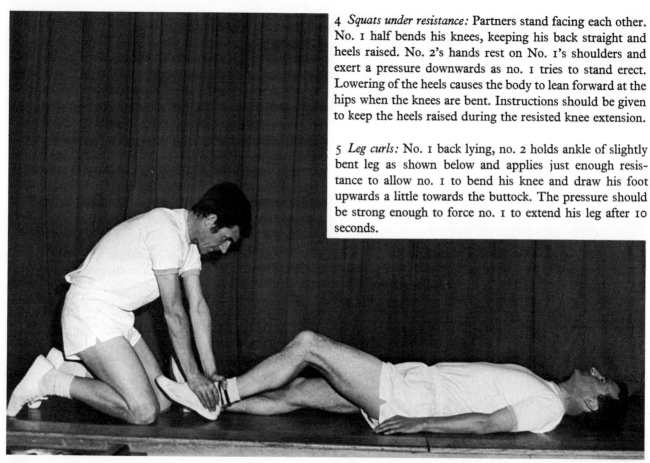

4 *Squats under resistance:* Partners stand facing each other. No. 1 half bends his knees, keeping his back straight and heels raised. No. 2's hands rest on No. 1's shoulders and exert a pressure downwards as no. 1 tries to stand erect. Lowering of the heels causes the body to lean forward at the hips when the knees are bent. Instructions should be given to keep the heels raised during the resisted knee extension.

5 *Leg curls:* No. 1 back lying, no. 2 holds ankle of slightly bent leg as shown below and applies just enough resistance to allow no. 1 to bend his knee and draw his foot upwards a little towards the buttock. The pressure should be strong enough to force no. 1 to extend his leg after 10 seconds.

17 Skill to utilise strength and stamina

THERE COMES a time when further gains in strength and stamina are of little value unless the performer has the skill to utilise fully his physical capability. If this skill is not adequately developed then more time should be spent on skill training than on physical conditioning. Only practice can produce a standard of performance that is consistently of a high standard.

Every basic skill has to be learned until it can be done automatically, without conscious effort. Watch a young child's first attempts to feed itself. The spoon is filled laboriously, carried jerkily to the face and emptied somewhere approaching the open mouth. More often than not the food slops over the chin, bib and chair. In time, more of each spoonful passes between the lips, the movement becomes more adept and less concentration is evident.

Parents talk of these fundamental activities as skills which the child has learned, as stages of its development. 'He is crawling, walking, feeding himself now . . .' and so on, are the phrases used as the child matures. They also talk of skilled craftsmen, skilful footballers, and the skill of the surgeon. The term 'skill' then is used to describe the ability to achieve a high standard of performance consistently.

Factors affecting the acquisition of skill

In sport there are men and women who succeed despite glaring deficiencies in their repertoire of skill, and it is difficult to be dogmatic when discussing the relative importance of all the factors which contribute to or impair skilful performance. We speak of natural ability, environment, body type, coaching, practice, and most important of all, motivation—the compelling desire to be good, to dominate all others. 'All I ever wanted to be was a good dancer,' says Maya Plisetskaya, Bolshoi's Prima Ballerina. Substitute 'footballer', 'runner', 'golfer' or 'swimmer' and you will find the same phrase in the life stories of the stars of these sports. But what about the other factors just mentioned? They need further consideration before being acceptable as gospel. Let us take a closer look at them.

Natural ability

'He is a natural.' We speak of a man with a natural bent for ball games, or with an innate ability for running. Some men and boys do tend to have more of an aptitude for one sport than another. It may be due to body type, mental outlook and previous experience, but whatever the reason they should be encouraged to practise the sports at which they are likely to succeed and to maintain an interest in them until late in life.

But sometimes men and boys want to take up sports which may at first sight appear to be unsuitable for them, beyond their natural ability. Before throwing cold water on such aspirations the coach and schoolmaster should remember that many champions have succeeded despite physical disabilities and that it is the inner compulsion to succeed coupled with the determination to practice that counts for most in the acquisition of skill.

Another consideration to allow for is the 'late developer'. It is easy to get the wrong idea of a boy's ability, to think that he has no natural bent towards games when in fact it may be nothing more than lack of opportunity in the past for practice. For example, there is almost bound to be a wide difference in sports ability between boys joining a secondary school from a junior one blessed with masters keen on sport and those coming from a smaller one with perhaps older and less agile teachers taking sport. The boys who have had more competition and experience can all too easily be regarded as having 'natural ability', whilst the 'late developers' may be ignored as having little aptitude. The good ones should not be favoured by coaching reserved for teams representing the house or lower school. It could so easily happen that the 'late developer', getting off to a poor start, is penalised throughout his schooldays by this kind of preferential treatment.

Age

The ability to play different sports varies according to the age of the pupil and the physical requirements of the particular sport. Ice skaters, skiers and swimmers tend to start young (both girls and boys)—when five or six years old.

Team games cannot be taught successfully to boys until they reach the age of eleven. They can play a kind of football in which two sides chase a ball all over the field, but positional play demands an appreciation of team-work which does not usually develop until the eleventh year. Occasionally there are exceptions such as Pele who, even as a boy of eleven playing with men, had the uncanny ability to plot elaborate offensive moves on the spur of the moment. He was a skinny, undernourished bootblack but obsessed with football. At sixteen he played his first game with Santos, Brazil, and scored four goals. His exceptional ability earned him the title 'King of Soccer' and made him a millionaire.

But few boys have such an intense passion for soccer as Pele and it is pointless to thrust a boy at a sport until he is mentally ready to enjoy it; the desire to play and train must come first from within. There is always a temptation for fathers and coaches to lead a boy into a particular sport because it is a tradition with the family or district, but boys who are made to play and practise before they are old enough to enjoy it may develop a dislike for the game which stays all their life. On the other hand some boys who start to play their father's sport when very young grow up to be as good, if not better, than the father himself.

In the early teens there is a tendency for boys to concentrate upon the sports at which they excel but until then they should be exposed to as many games and recreations as possible so that the decision to specialise can be made upon a wide background of experience and according to individual inclination. The value of practice and training for greater skill will then be more evident and acceptable.

Tradition and environment

Hero worship is a great teacher. Boys put their players on a pedestal of perfection, copy their mannerisms and even adopt their names in casual games. Take away the opportunity to see first-class players in action and you would see a different style of play emerging. Before television reception had reached the Isle of Man there was a noticeable difference in the football and cricket boys played there, for example, than that played in schools in Old Trafford, Manchester, where boys had ample opportunity to see good players and to become infused with the enthusiasm which abounds around the famous grounds of Manchester United and Lancashire County Cricket Club. Visits to see good performers are well worthwhile for skill learning and also for stimulating motivation.

There must be something about environment. How else can you explain the reputation Battersea maintains for good boxers, South Wales for Rugby and Motherwell for champion swimmers? Once the interest has been kindled by rubbing shoulders with celebrities the talent develops and is not allowed to pass unnoticed, for coaches spring from the older players who bring on the promising young ones.

Temperament

Differences in mental outlook make men and boys pursue different sports. Whilst one prefers the rugged body-contact sport such as rugby another is much happier playing a less boisterous one demanding finer skills and closer concentration. No doubt, skill develops more rapidly when an individual is deeply interested in a game he has himself chosen and for which he is both mentally and physically suited.

Body type and physique

Studies have been made of the body types of Olympic athletes and it does appear that at some sports men with a certain type of physique excel, whilst in other games, and Association Football is a notable example, there is a wide variety of physiques among the top players. Chapter 19 deals with the implications of body build with regard to performance at sport and to general health.

Practice

By continuous practice a player begins to 'feel' the whole movement so precisely that he knows immediately whether his own performance is good or bad. It has been said that practice and motivation are the most important factors influencing the acquisition of skill. But what type of practice? When should it start and how long should the periods be? It is a subject in itself and has therefore been left for chapter 18.

18 Skill practice and training

THE IMMORTAL Bobby Jones,[1] who will always be remembered by golfers for achieving the 'Impregnable Quadrilateral'—winning the British Amateur title, the British Open title, the American Amateur title and the American Open title in the same year, a feat that is unlikely to be repeated—says that the only thing that matters in golf is that you hit the ball with no more self-consciousness than goes with chopping wood, throwing stones or beating rugs.

Certain skills tend to be lost when conscious thought is given to them. Witness the player who has lost confidence and tries too hard—he often makes a bigger mess of his game than ever, because by thinking too much about a stroke he is interfering with a natural reflex pattern. Physiologists write that in the beginning the movements of any skill are controlled by conscious thought in the pre-motor area of the cerebrum but with practice the co-ordination is taken over as a reflex movement by the cerebellum. Any adjustments needed to compensate for changing circumstances in a game—such as the distance of the golf ball from the hole, the football from the goal, the speed of a centre or the position of tackling players—are also catered for by reflex adjustments initiated by the cerebellum. Ultimately, with continued practice in actual match conditions, judgement and anticipation improve to such a pitch that very little conscious effort is needed. It becomes, in fact, as easy as chopping wood.

But there are many forms of practice. Mere repetition of the movements does not necessarily bring improvement, and without doubt during the early stages of learning a new skill the best form of practice is that done under expert supervision. By playing the game, both good and bad habits are formed, and no matter whether it be an industrial or a sports skill being learned, experience and tests have shown that it is far more difficult to remove bad habits than it is to teach the skill from scratch. The danger to watch is that during the early stages of teaching a new skill, the interest of the player is not quenched by the frustration of not being allowed to try the activity and find things out for himself. On the contrary, experimentation should be encouraged and intervention by the coach be left for those moments when an explanation or small demonstration is needed to give the beginner the right feeling and the key to the whole activity.

After the early stages of learning have been completed less supervision by the coach is needed, and when the beginner has the right feeling for the movement, much may be gained from watching really top-class performers in action, both in the flesh and on film. By these additional aids the novice's understanding of the skill is increased and he begins to make more progress from his own trials.

When he has watched Bobby Charlton feint to the left to draw the defence, then jig to the right before chipping the ball neatly on to Denis Law's forehead, a boy wants to try it himself in the next match. It may not come off but what does it matter? He has learned something from the original display and his own attempts afterwards. In time the technique will come.

Sometimes competition can help to stimulate the urge to train harder and play better but here too there is a pitfall for the unwary to watch. Once a man or boy has got used to the idea of winning he may not be keen to risk losing a match by trying new shots nor may he relish altering his style even though it could ultimately raise his level of performance. Thus, the junior tennis champion may fall back on safety play when in difficulties against a rising player. An extreme example of such safety-first tactics is often evident on a school Sports Day when one of the better junior high jumpers, who has used straddle style for most of the competition, reverts to scissors after a failure when the bar is approaching his limit because he knows he can clear for certain with scissors a height good enough to win. He may know that scissors style can never carry him to a top-notch standard but unless given firm advice and encouragement to persevere with straddle style he is likely to revert.

Although competition has this inherent danger of falling

back on safety-first tactics, no competition at all is not the way to build champion performance, for it is one matter serving an ace in a Saturday afternoon tennis 'knock-up' and a far different one at match point in a critical tournament game. Practice must go hand-in-hand with graded competition with all its stresses and battles.

Competition should not be so stiff that a player is trounced and discouraged, nor too easy to allow victory without a battle. Through practice in training and play in competition, skill can become so well conditioned that despite the tenseness of the situation a consistently high standard of performance can be maintained.

A question hotly debated is that of how long a skill practice period should last. If a player has to perform the skills of the game during competition at times when he is physically fatigued then he should also experience the movements of the activity whilst fatigued during practice. But when a player begins to feel tired he is inclined to make half-hearted efforts, lose concentration and begin to repeat faults of style which may, in time, become ingrained. The time spent practising is then more harmful than no practice at all.

One form of skill practice deserves special mention. It is called 'pressure training', through which intensive practice of particular skills can be assured during a training session. It has been used extensively as a soccer coaching device and Walter Winterbottom, former chief coach to the Football Association and former Manager of the England football team, recommends it highly. In his book *Soccer Coaching*[2] many 'pressure-training' techniques are described, such as the centre forward's practice at shooting first time as balls are rolled to him first from one wing and then the other. He is continuously running up to a ball, shooting, turning, running on to another, shooting again, running back and so on. It helps to make him perform automatically without time for conscious thought—a condition which he will have to meet many times during a match. In such ways players can learn to assess situations automatically—the bounce of the ball, the wind, proximity of other players—and make the necessary adjustments by reflex action.

To sum up, practice does not make perfect, but permanent. Practice of the right type can ingrain an ability so that a consistently high standard is reached.

Coaching

'A little picture is worth a thousand words' runs an old Chinese proverb and this is especially true of teaching a new skill. Let the group or individual see the complete performance first: with no talking and no other distractions to diminish the impact of the demonstration on the senses.

Pupils need to have a clear concept of what they are going to attempt and this visual impression can be most vividly conveyed by seeing an expert in actual competition rather than by giving a special demonstration. Sometimes a man demonstrating shows the audience what he thinks he does rather than what he actually does in competition when all his effort is directed towards achieving a winning performance: he is not thinking then about body movements.

After the initial introduction of a skill it is very important that beginners be allowed to try and emulate what they have just seen.

Immediate practice helps them to understand what is required and to realise their own abilities. It takes a trial before a pupil realises 'that it is not as easy as it looks'. Furthermore, through trying to master the skill they often deepen the desire to play well. They enjoy the practice and the satisfaction it gives them.

During the time when the group is freely practising, the coach can assess ability and decide upon the form his instruction will next take. In some sports the skill may have to be broken down into smaller and more readily assimilated skills so that each part can be mastered separately before being joined together as a complete activity. The discus throw can be taught by practising the throw from the standing position, then when that has been grasped, the turn can be learned. Finally when the athlete is competent in both skills, the parts can be put together and practised.

But in other sports the coach might decide that verbal correction and practice of the whole skill is the method best suited to the class according to their performance in their first attempts at the activity.

In fact the success of a coach depends to a great extent upon this ability to analyse performance and detect the difficulties which may be impeding individual progress. He does not try merely to make his charges into carbon copies of a champion they have seen demonstrating. Stars in sport invariably have their own peculiarities of style due to temperament and physique. Rather must the coach recognise the right technique as it emerges from a beginner's early efforts. He must praise it as progress is made and nurse it along carefully until a consistently successful style develops: one that will not limit potentiality for progress in the future.

Match conditions

It is easy to see that there is a world of difference between trapping a softly inflated football in a gymnasium when wearing plimsolls and trapping a ball when about to be tackled by a bustling defender. Match practice then must be the aim of all skill training, but whilst recognising the need for practice under actual competitive conditions the coach must not ignore altogether the value of practice in particular skills as a special part of the training programme. Sometimes the situations for the practice of certain skills have to be artificially arranged so that adequate experience and practice is gained. For example, in a game of football a centre forward may have only three or four chances to hit a low cross from the wing but these are the vital moments of the game, the opportunity for which all the team have been working and the centre forward must be able to shoot accurately each time. He must, therefore, practise this skill at other times than in the course of a match.

The skill has to be ingrained by concentrated and intensive periods of training so that the shot becomes a reflex action to a given set of circumstances: the speed of the crossing ball, its height from the ground and distance from the goal. The body lean and position of the feet are all controlled by reflex computation and if the ball finishes in the back of the net it is not the result of conscious control at the time but concentrated practice in training for the opportunity to arise.

Similarly, the mere practice or playing of a game does not develop every aspect of agility, strength and stamina which make for star performance because during the normal course of a game the need for these qualities of fitness only arises at infrequent intervals. Consequently the coach must be able to assess a player's physical ability and prescribe appropriate training.

and more likely to hit the unsuccessful than the successful athlete or player.

If he is off form for some unaccountable reason, the remedy is not to go on light training but to introduce a change of routine—a complete break from work, play, competition and training. Exhortations to work harder, to 'stick at it' are rarely as effective as the mental refreshment derived from a few days' holiday. After such a refreshing relaxation of routine the sportsman often comes back to his schedule with renewed zest. The coach must make the decision whether to press on through a poor period or to recommend a rest. There is no hard-and-fast rule.

Being a coach is no simple task, he has to be a psychologist as well as a trainer of fitness and skill. What suits one may not be effective with another. Perhaps this is one reason why some of the South American soccer teams now have their own fully qualified club psychologist travelling with them on World Cup tournaments.

Is it the coach or the athlete that gets stale?

The argument against intensive training used to be that too much training made a sportsman 'stale'. But the rigorous training schedules followed by those who reach the top today makes nonsense of this excuse to ease off training. 'Staleness' is now considered to be more of an attitude of mind rather than a physical condition. It is akin to boredom

REFERENCES
1 Bobby Jones, *Golf is my Game* (Chatto and Windus).
2 Walter Winterbottom, *Soccer Coaching* (Football Association).

19 Sports to suit the body type

YOU CANNOT make a silk purse out of a sow's ear but you can make the most of what you've got. Some people are cut out to run a four-minute mile, others to swim the Channel or to be a Mr Universe or play at Twickenham. By looking at an athlete's type of body, it is almost possible to predict in which direction his sporting future lies. No matter how hard he tried, the tall thin greyhound type of man could never walk on to the rostrum for the title of Mr Universe. Nor, on the other hand, is Mr Universe likely to win an Olympic gold medal for the 10 000 metres. Sportsmen should have a good look at the three body types described below before starting serious training. Remember though that it is not possible to classify everyone accurately into one particular class. There are no clearly cut divisions. Most men fall in between the different groups and there is always the exception in sport to prove the rule.

Classification into body types

There is no such person as the average man, mentally, socially or physically. Yet we often use the phrase casually in conversation. Physically, men differ greatly from one another according to their body structure: the length of bone, amount of fatty tissue and degree of muscularity.

It is generally agreed that there are three different basic body types. They go under a variety of names from Greyhound, Ape and Hippopotamus to Aesthenic, Athletic, and Pyknic or, in medical jargon, ectomorphic, mesomorphic and endomorphic, different names all describing the three fundamental body types. The physiologists agree on the characteristics of each type which are broadly as follows:

1 *Hippopotamus or endomorph:* The typical picture of the extreme endomorph shows a ponderous, soft-fleshed man, broad and of medium height. His shoulders are big and strong but giving a rounded cut, rather than square, to his figure. He tends to become excessively fat and, as a direct result, is more susceptible to the serious organic diseases such as heart disorders, high blood pressure and other digestive and respiratory malfunctions. The average expectancy of life of endomorphs is generally less than that of the other two groups. A simple guide to endomorphic characteristics is the circumference of the girth as compared with the chest. The insurance companies heavily penalise those with a greater waist measurement than chest by demanding higher premiums for life insurance.

But sometimes the endomorph is in reality the muscular athlete who has, through laziness, gluttony and inactivity, run to fat. But if he is basically a mesomorph, he will respond to rehabilitative exercise and diet better than the true endomorph. It is never too late to mend.

In sport the heavy endomorph has spheres in which he can outstrip the other body types. In long-distance swimming, water polo and cycling there are many world champions with this body build. Most of the world's best weight lifters and wrestlers are endomorphic-mesomorphs.

Socially, the big endomorph is usually well adapted and liked. He can derive a great deal of physical, mental and psychological satisfaction from participating in sports and physical recreations of a more social nature such as sailing, canoeing, riding, tennis and bowls.

2 *Ape or mesomorph:* His dominant physical characteristic is his well-developed musculature. Broad shoulders are linked to a strong neck by tapering trapezii muscles whilst from below the shoulders to the waist the latissimus dorsi can be seen giving a wedge-like appearance to the upper body. When the ape type are fit, they have little superfluous fat, but in middle life it may become difficult to differentiate between the fatter mesomorph and the true endomorph. But provided that exercise is continued and diet carefully watched, this type of man maintains his energetic approach to work and sport and is likely to avoid most ailments.

Mesomorphic men excel in the robust body-contact games where speed, strength, power and endurance are all required. You can see them packing in the scrum, or on the soccer pitch, or sprinting and throwing in athletic meetings. They train hard and are said to be as determined to succeed in work as they are in play.

3 *Greyhound or ectomorph:* These are the tall, angular, thin people with only a sparse covering of fat and muscle tissue on their prominent bones. The neck, trunk and limbs are long and thin; the ribs stick out prominently. The general muscular development appears to be poor and gives a false impression of frailty. Yet these are the ones who, according to the insurance statistics, live the longest and who are normally free from the more serious and chronic organic diseases. The only dangers they face are those of respiratory infections and nervous disorders. If they can avoid being run-down mentally and physically and are not exposed to under-nourishment, cold and damp, they are likely to be able to attend the funerals of their endo- and mesomorphic friends.

In sports and games their physical capacity enables them to succeed more in the non-body-contact games such as basketball, tennis and cricket. They can also do better than most in the middle- and long-distance running events.

Method of classification into body types

Most methods classify by numbers. One of the best known is that devised by Dr Sheldon, who used photographic charting procedures together with anatomical measurements made with tape-measure and callipers which pick up super-fluous fat from the muscle just as you would pinch it with the forefinger and thumb. He worked out a seven-point scale for each characteristic of body type—fatty tissue, muscle, and bone. An extremely fat endomorph would score seven for his fat, one for muscle and one for bone; his rating would be 711 (seven one one, not seven hundred and eleven). An extremely thin ectomorph would score one for the dominance of fat in his build, perhaps one for muscle and seven for bone. His rating would be 117. But extreme cases are fortunately rare and the ratings most frequently found are in the region of 443, 344 and 235.

It is worth trying to understand the relative fitness and aptitude of the different body types. Far better is it that a young man's enthusiasm and ambitions be guided towards an aim that he is able to reach rather than see him frustrated by lack of progress in an activity for which he is not physically suited. This is primarily the job of the physical education specialist in schools and of coaches in clubs. Individuals react differently to training; some will reach the heights of international success, others will have to be content with the satisfaction of achieving victories in the area, county or club competition, or with the enjoyment from having played as well as possible against good opposition.

20 Exercise and health

Guinness is good for you, proclaim the posters. *Beer is best.* Can we be equally dogmatic about health and physical fitness and say, *Exercise is good for you*? There can be no doubt that in most cases the answer would be *yes*. But before reaching that conclusion it would be as well to examine what really constitutes a condition of physical fitness, to consider how important exercise really is compared with all the other factors influencing health, and to weigh in the balance of judgement the effects of exercise. It is mainly a matter of looking at the complete picture and seeing exercise in its proper perspective. When this has been done there should be little doubt that exercise is good for you.

The attributes of physical fitness

Perhaps the most important of all the attributes of good health and physical fitness is the ability to resist infection and sickness. Living conditions, work, habits, leisure-time activities and domestic environment all have their physical and psychological effects on this constitutional capacity.

Exercise through work or leisure activities is one of the important factors in maintaining health.

The other major attributes of fitness are more easily defined. In a true condition of physical fitness they are all in a state of advanced development. To list them briefly they are:

1 *Strength:* The muscular ability to exert a force against some external resistance; to push, pull or carry a heavy object. It is dependent upon muscle bulk, neuro-muscular control, strong bones, firm joints and tough ligaments.

2 *Power:* Often this term is confused with strength. But power involves the exertion of a strong contraction within a given period of time. It could be represented thus:

$$\text{Strength} \times \text{speed} = \text{power}$$

Power, as the name implies, is usually a dynamic explosive release of force, as for example when a boxer punches a heavy bag or an athlete puts the shot.

3 *Endurance:* The ability to carry on physical activity for long periods before the onset of fatigue is usually described as endurance. Neuro-muscular endurance is one aspect of total endurance which is affected by the efficiency of all the body's systems and by the determination to keep going.

4 *Mobility:* Suppleness is synonymous with youth and stiffness is a sign of old age. The ability to move all limbs and the spine gracefully through a wide range of movement is an essential attribute of physical fitness.

5 *Neuro-muscular control:* This is the co-ordination of muscular contraction and relaxation to effect a smooth and accurate pattern of movement. When control is poor owing to nervous disorders or lack of skill, movements are jerky and lack precision. Good control is expressed in the quality of style and grace.

Purposely left to the end is the one attribute which influences all others—motivation. Most physical factors can be improved when the motivation is strong. The influence of the mind, the motivating force behind all others, cannot be over-estimated. This will to live, the incentive to succeed, the motivating drive—call it what you will—is the greatest single factor upon which physical fitness depends. All the others respond to exercise—motivation develops from within.

The factors affecting physical fitness

There are many significant factors which contribute to, or detract from, physical health. Exercise is but one of these. Those who wish to be really fit must appreciate the significance of every one of the influences listed below, for effort spent in exercising can be cancelled out by neglect of other essentials.

Food: The first need of the under-developed and under-nourished weakling is not exercise but good food and rest. Without a plentiful and balanced supply of food for muscle building and energy fuel, the body uses its own tissue as fuel. It burns itself up. Although the intake of food may be adequate, if mealtimes are irregular digestive disorders can develop which adversely affect physical fitness.

Congenital health and physique: Some people can afford a fifty-guinea suit whilst others have to be content with one for a good deal less. There are also inequalities in the physique and health which we inherit and this of course has a marked effect on physical fitness.

Rest and sleep: No one can explain satisfactorily what happens when we sleep, but it is known that individuals vary in their requirements. Older people seem able to carry on an active life with little sleep and a series of 'cat-naps' throughout the day whereas many young athletes feel below par if they don't have a good ten hours each night. Unless individuals have sufficient sleep to allow the processes of physical and mental recuperation to take place, they will automatically function less efficiently; they will be less physically fit for the task to be done.

Mental and physical recreation: The term 'recreation' implied originally a rebuilding, a re-creation. There is a lot of truth in the old adage that a change is as good as a rest, for after a break in the routine everyone can return to the task in hand with renewed zest. Physical activity, especially when taken in the open air, can provide the means of letting off steam, of venting inhibitions and of giving expression to innate desires. Recreation in some form or other is part of living and affects the way we feel physically and mentally.

Consider the exhilaration that follows a good game and a rub-down afterwards. The world seems to be a better place. We are fitter if we feel fitter.

Habits and personal hygiene: In the daily Press frightening statistical evidence is available to show how over-eating, drinking alcohol and smoking can shorten the life-span and cause serious illnesses. It is a sad reflection that these so-called pleasures have to be regarded as direct causative agents in premature deaths from coronary thrombosis, kidney trouble and lung cancer.

Exercise: Physical exercise affects all the systems of the body. It stimulates them into increased activity. Following a natural law, these systems develop with use and degenerate with disuse. The many beneficial effects which result from regular exercise are examined in more detail below.

Effects of exercise

Vigorous exercise has a stimulating effect on some systems and depresses others. The circulatory and respiratory organs directly concerned in supplying the energy fuels of food and oxygen immediately increase their activity but the digestive organs partially or temporarily cease functioning in order that the resources of the body can be satisfactorily marshalled to meet the immediate demands of the muscles. After the exercise is finished the return to normal function is gradual and the speed at which recovery is made depends upon the general efficiency of the body to make good the oxygen debt incurred, to replace the simple food consumed and to eliminate the waste by-products of the exercise. 'Oxygen debt' is virtually the difference between the oxygen required in the performance of the exercise and the oxygen actually taken in. More oxygen is used than is currently breathed during the activity and consequently the heart and lungs have to continue working at a high rate after the exercise is finished. The time needed for the pulse rate to recover is often taken as an index of physical fitness. The fitter the man the quicker the pulse returns to normal. If the exercise in the form of regular training is repeated at intervals over a period of time, more permanent changes occur in the functional activity and structure of the organs affected. These effects are discussed in detail below.

THE EFFECTS ON THE CIRCULATORY SYSTEM

A marked increase in the heart rate is immediately noticeable when exercise begins. There is also a considerable increase in blood pressure due to the following causes:

1 The increased outward flow from the heart.

2 The quicker return of venous blood to the heart. This is mainly due to the massaging action of the muscles on the veins. The flow back is assisted by this squeezing effect.

3 The pumping action of the diaphragm. On each inspiration the diaphragm moves downwards and so increases the pressure in the abdomen and decreases that of the thorax. The blood then automatically passes from the higher pressure area into the lower.

The composition of the blood itself is not affected very much initially. Some athletes may be seen sucking glucose tablets immediately before a race in order to 'give themselves extra energy' or to maintain the balance of blood sugar. But in fact the normal concentration of glucose in the blood is not affected much unless the exercise is very arduous and prolonged, as for example in long-distance and marathon running. The liver carries its own store of glucose in the form of glycogen which is broken down and released into the blood as it passes through the liver during exercise. This stock is not significantly depleted by short athletic events.

The heart muscle responds to progressive resistance exercise in much the same way as do the skeletal muscles: it becomes bigger and stronger and becomes capable of greater output per beat. This enlargement is generally called 'hypertrophy'. Owing to the increased volume per stroke the resting heart rate becomes slower. For example, highly trained long-distance runners have heart rates as low as forty to forty-five per minute. They have therefore a wider range and reserve to call upon before reaching a maximum rate per minute. The effects of fatigue are consequently not felt as quickly with the trained as with the untrained man.

Graduated exercise has a marked beneficial effect for those overweight because it helps to break down fatty deposits of cholesterol clogging the circulatory system. If these deposits are allowed to build up on the inside walls of the arteries the bore becomes smaller and eventually a clot of blood sticks fast and the flow of blood stops. Coronary thrombosis is usually the result of over-indulgence in rich foods and alcohol, combined with lack of exercise.

THE EFFECTS ON THE RESPIRATORY SYSTEM

During exercise additional oxygen and energy fuel are required whilst lactic acid and carbon dioxide are formed. In order to provide more oxygen and to eliminate carbon dioxide, the rate and depth of respiration increases, thus exposing a greater area of the lung for the interchange of gases. The increase in rate and depth is entirely reflex and results mainly from the greater concentration of carbon dioxide in the blood acting chemically on the respiratory centre in the brain.

After long periods of the type of training which increases endurance, the normal rate of respiration decreases. The average rate for an untrained man is normally about twenty inspirations per minute, whereas the trained athlete may only breathe in eight times for the same amount of muscular activity.

The vital capacity—the amount of air the lungs can breathe in and out—increases after training so that a greater area of lung surface can be presented to the inspired air. This means that a greater proportion of gases can be exchanged in the same breath. Experiments with breathing apparatus have shown that a trained man will breathe in less air for the same given amount of work than an untrained man, which seems to indicate a more efficient system for absorbing oxygen. Training, then, improves efficiency for everyday work and potentiality for long periods of exhaustive work requiring respiratory stamina.

THE EFFECTS ON THE MUSCULAR SYSTEM

The effects of progressive resistance exercises on muscular strength has been discussed in chapter 1 in which the increases in size of the muscle fibres and total muscular bulk are briefly explained. The sarcolemma and connective tissue are similarly affected, growing thicker and stronger. The changes occurring within the muscle which enable it to sustain longer periods of exhaustive exercise are less easy to explain, for endurance does not depend entirely on strength. Exercises which specifically build stamina are more effective than strengthening exercises in training for events and sports needing endurance because they develop local endurance within particular muscle groups as well as the general endurance of the whole body. Endurance results from a chemical reaction within the muscle as well as the physical development of the muscle fibres.

The efficiency of the muscular system is affected by the strength, reciprocal relaxation, tone and length of the agonist and antagonist muscle groups. Balanced training programmes ensure a harmonious development of muscles in all these aspects.

THE EFFECTS ON THE ALIMENTARY SYSTEM

During periods of strenuous muscular effort, the activity of the digestive systems is initially depressed although later stimulated into increased activity. The peristaltic movements of the stomach are reduced and the blood vessels supplying the digestive organs are constricted so as to divert the blood to the muscles requiring nourishment and to the skin for cooling. A meal taken just before exercise lies heavily in the stomach and may cause symptoms of indigestion or, when the stomach is very full, impair respiration by hindering the downward movement of the diaphragm. When the body has recovered from a bout of strenuous exercise the digestive system becomes abnormally active as if to compensate for the period of inhibited depression during the performance of the exercise. This would tend to offset any possible deleterious effect through interruption of the normal digestive and assimilation processes. In fact regular exercise sharpens the appetite and tones up the whole digestive system. There are many other far-reaching immediate and secondary effects of exercise but the main ones have been discussed above. Suffice it merely to touch upon the others briefly. The body temperature rises slightly initially and then is maintained at a consistent level by the dilation of blood vessels in the skin and the cooling of the blood by exposure to the lower temperature of the cool air and the evaporating sweat. Fat people tend to be less efficient in keeping the body temperature down because the fatty tissue partially insulates the blood from the cooling process of the sweat evaporating on the skin.

From these bare facts on how exercise affects the mind and body there should emerge clearly the inescapable conclusion: muscles are there to be used, and when they are, the resulting effects are good.

21 Fitness after forty

'LIFE BEGINS at forty' runs the adage, but the insurance statisticians would add a rider: so does death. For the man, the forties are dangerous years. He shoulders more responsibility, works and worries more, frequently eats more and plays less. It all takes its toll. One of the biggest enemies of the over-forties is coronary thrombosis—it is the killer in their midst. The figures for this devastating illness are alarming; one person in six now dies of coronary thrombosis. Can anything be done to avoid this condition which strikes down people in the prime of life? There are new drugs now being used after an attack, but the greatest advance is being made in early diagnosis of the warning symptoms and avoidance of the predisposing causes.

A woman may be as old as she looks, but a man is as old as his arteries. Coronary thrombosis is usually a direct result of arteries hardening and becoming clogged with fatty deposits which restrict and finally block the flow of nutritious blood to the vital organs. When the heart muscle is deprived of its blood-supply, part of its tissue may die or it may stop beating altogether. Men are attacked in this way more often than women; the ratio is about five to one.

Coronary conditions thrive in the fat man and those former sportsmen not usually described as fat but overweight. High blood pressure, heart diseases, diabetes, gall bladder disorders and many forms of arthritis also flourish and are more prevalent in those who are overweight. It is important that men should recognise the great potentialities for harm in over-indulgence in rich foods, lack of exercise, and resulting obesity. There are, of course, some cases where obesity results from imbalance in the functioning of the thyroid and, in some instances, of the pituitary glands, but unquestionably it is the excess of calory intake over requirements that really matters. Exercise consumes some of the calories taken in and it also helps to break up the deposits of cholesterol lining the artery walls. On the other hand unaccustomed and violent exercise can be dangerous for those over forty.

There is no distinct line between youth and age, but as a rough boundary forty is the year to note. There are of course the seemingly ageless forty-five year olds who appear much younger, and physiologically may be younger, than many thirty-five year olds, but as a general rule forty is the age to start thinking about exercise. It is the time for careful conditioning programmes rather than sporadic bursts of furious activity on a squash court trying to show a younger opponent that there is still life in the old man. Not one person in a thousand would stop in the middle of a game because he felt he had had enough, but weight training can be planned to give just enough exercise and no more. It is gradual, progressive and safe because there is no one to beat. It is geared to each individual's ability. Over-indulgence in exercise can cause excessive tiredness and thereby increase susceptibility to illness, but there is also danger in 'hanging up your boots'. There should be no sudden change from an active sports life to one of sedentary spectator. The body becomes accustomed over the years to regular exercise. Eating and resting habits usually remain the same, but when further relaxation replaces physical recreation, that part of the food intake formerly consumed as fuel is likely to be stored between the muscle fibres and beneath the skin as superfluous fat. Statistics can be quoted to show how the expectancy of life reduces proportionately with every inch that the waist measurements exceed those of the chest.

Perhaps one of the greatest failings of school physical education programmes during the last twenty or thirty years is that they have not inculcated habits of exercise in the young which have been retained during middle age. Perhaps too much emphasis has been placed on team games so that the player who finally realises in his thirties that he is a drag on his team and retires from the game has no individual sport to take the place of the team activity. Consequently he drives the family to the shops or potters about the garden on a Saturday afternoon or sits with thousands of others and takes pleasure from watching younger players in action. The position appears to get worse each year. Clubs experience more and more difficulty in finding players. Where four teams were once fielded only one or two can now be seen. This kind of social change is marked amongst the junior amateur football leagues. Whole leagues have disappeared after an existence of forty years.

Gradually the muscles of the thirty- or forty-year-old chairborne athlete begin to atrophy. They waste away like all things which are left abandoned. Other degenerative changes begin to appear, bringing limitations to leading a full life. Long periods of sitting at a desk, or worse still slumped in the driving seat of a car, eventually weaken and stretch the longitudinal muscles and ligaments of the back. The usual warning signs of pain occur and are often dismissed with a little joke about lumbago and the old man cracking up. Progressively the back becomes weaker and the pain more chronic. It has been estimated by a leading specialist in lumbar disc lesions that there is not one street or small community in Britain which does not have its martyr to lumbago. It is probable that many sufferers will have run through the gamut of treatment from general practitioner, orthopaedic specialist, physiotherapist, osteopath and bone-setter before finally becoming resigned to the affliction and learning to live with it. Unfortunately disc trouble tends to recur—far better to avoid injury by maintaining strong muscles in the back and avoiding as far as possible the lifting movements with a rounded back which render the muscles and ligaments susceptible to injury. Learning to live with backache can be a painful process when the only pain-free position may be to lie face downwards on a couch.

As it was at the beginning. Two men mark the ageless Matthews unsuccessfully in his last appearance for Blackpool v. Arsenal at Highbury. Matthews at forty-six, after thirty years in soccer, started a new career with his old club, Stoke City. His first game attracted an extra 26000 fans!

The protruding paunch may not only be a result of over-eating but also from slumping in a chair so that the upper body sags and rests on the mid section, pushing it out. A more erect sitting posture does not subject the abdomen to such pressure. The weight of the upper body is supported by the spine and the dorsal muscles. Exercises can keep the longitudinal, oblique and transverse muscles short and strong and so maintain the front abdominal wall in its proper place. Once this wall sags, the contents of the abdomen slip forward and digestive disorders often associated with a pot belly arise. The trunk curl should be a regular daily exercise for the over-forties. The exercise often done is the leg lift from back lying, but this exercise works the abdominal muscles in a lengthened condition and can cause the already stretched and weakened muscles to stretch still more and allow the abdomen to protrude even further.

Many sportsmen, especially soccer and rugby players, have injured knees at some time or other during their playing careers. Once training for the game stops, the quadriceps muscles of the thigh begin to waste. The speed at which the vastus medialis part of the quadriceps muscle wastes is more rapid. Weakened muscles do not adequately support a damaged knee joint and they allow too much laxity in walking. Each time the leg is swung forward the knee joint opens slightly as the tibia drops away from the femur, thus when the body weight is placed on to the forward leg, the two ends come together with a jar. Recurrent jarring of previously damaged joints is often the cause of accelerating the degenerative arthritic changes. It is a vicious circle—the weaker the muscle, the greater is the jarring and the cause of pain and swelling which in turn leads to the leg being rested from exercise and to eventually weaker muscles. And so the circle moves on. A pessimistic picture? It is not exaggerated. There has been no satisfactory explanation of the causes of arthritis, but the two main predisposing conditions for arthritis of the knee are weak quadriceps associated with an old injury to the joint. But exercise, particularly with weights, can help even chronic sufferers from arthritis of the knee. Men and women in their seventies who have severe osteo-arthritis of the knees are now finding relief from progressive resistance exercises. Before exercise started some of the patients were unable to walk up and down stairs normally. After six weeks many of them could. Some of them regained almost a full range of movement in their knee joints and could tackle jobs like gardening without pain, whereas before treatment this sort of activity was impossible. If aged patients can use weights in hospitals and National Health Rehabilitation Centres, what risk is there for the average man exercising after forty? The greatest risk is probably for those with impaired coronary circulation who do not realise their limitations, but there is danger for them too in shovelling snow, lifting heavy furniture or making a rock garden. The over-forties must think about their exercise and watch its effects. Excessive fatigue, rapid increases in respiration and pain are the warning signs which must be heeded. An annual check by the doctor is worthwhile. It is carried out in the armed services and also now in many of the large industrial organisations which place a high premium on physical fitness. Years of training and experience are wasted if a man dies in his forties. Leaders and executives are selected from this age-group and one of the important qualities considered in selection is physical fitness. Does the man have an energetic approach to his work? Does he look fit and active enough to drive the programme forward? Is he going to be absent through sickness? These are the questions that selection boards must consider. From a career and health point of view exercise can be a great benefit. Up to the age of forty, personal inclination and environment decide what sports are played but after forty other factors must be considered. These are discussed in greater detail in my book, *Fitness after Forty*,[1] which provides a practical guide for men and women who want to be fit after forty—fit to enjoy the best years of their lives.

REFERENCE

1 Eric Taylor, *Fitness after Forty* (John Murray).

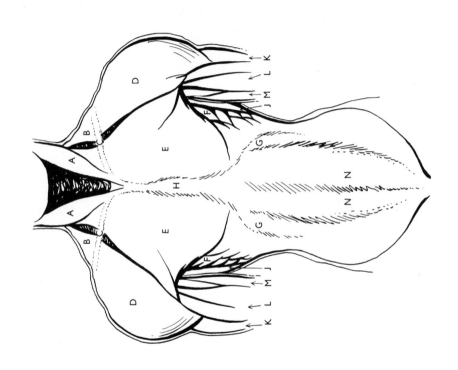

Muscles of trunk and shoulder girdle from the front

A Sternomastoid
B Trapezius
C Clavicle
D Deltoid
E Pectoralis major

F Serratus anterior
G External oblique
H Sternum
J Latissimus dorsi
K Brachialis

L Biceps brachialis
M Triceps (long head)
N Rectus abdominis
   covered by
   aponeurosis

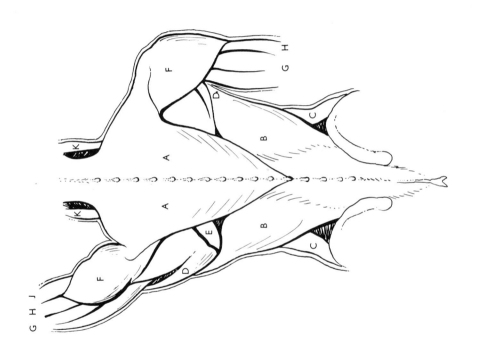

Muscles of trunk and shoulder girdle from behind

A Trapezius
B Latissimus dorsi
C External oblique
D Teres major
E Rhomboideus major
F Deltoid
G Triceps
H Brachialis
J Biceps brachialis
K Sternomastoid

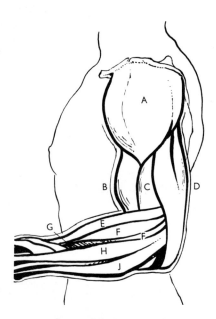

Arm and forearm muscles

A Deltoid
B Biceps brachialis
C Brachialis
D Triceps
E Brachioradialis
F, G and J Extensors of the wrist
H Long extensor of fingers

A Rectus femoris of quadriceps
B Outer head of quadriceps
C Inner head of quadriceps
D Anterior tibial muscle
E Inner edge of gastrocnemius
F Inner edge of soleus
G Sartorius

Thigh and leg muscles from the front

A Gluteus medius
B Gluteus maximus
C Broad fascia of the thigh
D Short head of biceps femoris
E Long head of biceps femoris
F Semitendinosus
G Semimembranosus
H Adductor magnus
J (Gracilis)
K Sartorius
L Gastrocnemius
M Soleus
N Peroneus longus
O Peroneus brevis
P Long flexor of the toes
Q Posterior tibial muscle

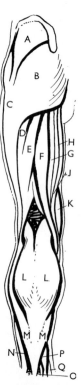

Thigh and leg muscles from behind